THE LOVE AROUND US

THE LOVE AROUND US

some haiku-inspired essays
to brighten your day

· · · • · · ·

Laura Lee Bond

ISBN 978-1-7360965-0-5 (Paperback)
ISBN 978-1-7360965-1-2 (Ebook)

Library of Congress Control Number 2020922344

Cover and book design by Seth & Laura Lee Bond
Author photo by Seth Bond

Printed and bound in the USA

First Printing January 2021

Visit www.LauraLeeBond.com

in the beginning
was great, deep, abiding love
timeless as heaven

CONTENTS

NATURE

PURE QUIRK

ALL THE LOVE AROUND US

By Way of Introduction

do something you love
for today and every day
ripples in a pond

IN 2007, ON A WHIM, I started submitting my Thursday time sheet with a haiku meant for my coworker in HR. When I left that job, I took the weekly practice with me. Every Thursday since 2008, I've sent a haiku to a list of friends, family, and friends of friends. Weeks when my writing practice was strong, I'd publish an essay to go with it. Over 600 haiku and several dozen essays later, I thought perhaps now might be a good time to share them outside of my little-traveled blog.

The essays span the acreage of my life—most were written between 2008 and 2020. They range from unemployment, depression, and fear of the unknown, to creativity, whimsy, and most importantly, love. Love of family, friends, and life. Wending its way through them all is a thread of hope.

In order to make the title of the book a haiku (thanks Susie!), I had to leave off a word I really wanted to include:

The Love Around Us

All. All the love around us, there is so much of it in both the momentous and mundane. Writing is my way of attempting to give this love a voice—my ripple in the pond.

Laura Lee (you can call me Lalee*) Bond
*Sounds like lollipop.

ISOLATED

Virtual Hugs

wanting to reach out
you seemed in need of a hug
I'm sorry we can't

A FRIEND AT WORK is going through a really hard time. We've been in the habit of giving one another hugs as needed. Today one was needed, but we couldn't partake. This thwarted encounter reminded me how isolating the pandemic is, which naturally made me think of other times I've felt this way. So, I thought I'd dust off a haiku from 2008 and an accompanying essay from 2012 to share.

... •...

a snowflake melted
on my lip it tasted of
lonely solitude

I MOVED TO DENVER in February 2000. It was a terribly lonely time for me. I had wanted to stay in Arizona to be near my family. But, I wasn't able to secure a full-time position in my chosen field and so had to move two states away. It was the second winter I was there, living in an apartment fifteen-minute walking distance from a job I could barely stand. A cold wind was blowing snowflakes around and while waiting for the crosswalk light to change, thinking of nothing in particular, a snowflake landed on my lower lip and melted. Its touch and subsequent melting were so quick and intimate—an unexpected kiss—I began to cry. It had been months since I'd felt the touch of another person, let alone a kiss. This profound loneliness reminded me of another time I'd gone months without human contact while living in Washington, DC.

··· •···

I HADN'T BEEN IN THE NATION'S CAPITAL LONG. It was a dusky fall evening when I walked home from my job in the Economics Department at The George Washington University where I'd recently started work on my Masters of Museum Studies. I'd come up Connecticut Avenue and passed by the south entrance to Metro located directly under Dupont Circle. As I entered the park, I remember looking at the sky turning that beautiful Prussian blue thinking, *See? Same great sky, it's not so different from home.*

But I was homesick. I missed seeing people I knew. I missed saying hello to them when I walked through town. I missed knowing the person who served me a scone and coffee in the morning. I hated to admit it, but I was lonely. At that moment, as I was crossing the fountain in the center of the circular park, I felt so supremely lonely I wanted to cry.

I was just past the edge of the huge fountain when I heard someone shout, "Hey!" which I naturally ignored.

Crazy yelling people were nothing new to the District, especially in Dupont Circle, and I was learning to become inured to them.

Again I heard "Hey!" followed by, "Is that a Macy's Coffee House mug?" I paused, remembering the to-go mug attached to the outside of my backpack, a habit I'd picked up in my small town.

I started to turn as the voice continued, "From Flagstaff, Arizona?!" It carried more than a hint of the incredulous. At this, I spun around to fully see the voice.

It belonged to a man, of unknown age, but obvious unusual character. A face that had seen the '60s but probably didn't remember it as such. The face wore glasses and was framed by shoulder-length slightly stringy long hair. There was kindness there. He was seated on the side of the fountain. Bumper stickers of all sorts covered an open guitar case next to him.

The guitar perched casually in his lap, he continued his query. "Have you been to Macy's?!" he asked excitedly.

I answered as I walked back towards him, "Not only have I been to Macy's, but I've worked there." I smiled at the stranger in spite of myself, noticing that one of the bumper stickers read, "Play that Funky Music White Boy."

5

"You're from Flagstaff!" His voice almost cracked at this last sentence.

"I am!" I replied enthusiastically, despite myself. "Are you?!"

"I am—I used to live there—you probably served me coffee!"

I squinted at him, cocking my head to the left. "You do look a little familiar ..."

"I'm Gage!" he pulled out his driver's license for me to inspect. "I looked more like this when I lived there." The photo indicated a man who had about twenty more pounds on him and possibly a few more showers.

"YEAH!" I shouted. "Yeah! I recognize you now. WOW. I can't believe you recognized the Macy's mug!" I handed his license back.

"I was just sitting here, thinking about Flagstaff and how much I missed it and I looked up and couldn't believe I saw a Macy's mug on your backpack. I had to call to you." There were tears in his eyes. I recognized that feeling and my own eyes teared up, remembering what I'd just been thinking about as I crossed the park.

"Wow," I said profoundly, knowing that he'd understand all the meaning behind the word.

We spent the next thirty-five minutes chatting about Flagstaff, our lives, how we'd ended up in DC, what we thought of it. We hugged like old friends. Both of our eyes were damp from tears. We laughed the laughter of nervous relief to have found someone else we could relate to in the city that had seemed so overwhelming to us both. We exchanged numbers.

We never met again.

The meeting was a gift to us both at a moment when we'd needed it most. Its importance and significance was not lost on us. I am grateful to this day for all the little twists and turns life put us both through in order to meet up on that fall evening under the great dusky sky in the whole wide amazing world.

WORD FRIPPERY

A First

Thursday is the day
next to Friday but better
for the hope it holds

MONDAY IS FULL OF THE DREARY and bleary-eyed shuffling back to work. Monday is defiant and surly, coffee stained and a tad bitter. Wouldn't you be if you were bullied by the memory of Saturday and Sunday? Monday sulks in and kicks you to wake up because that's how they've been treated for decades. Monday is an androgynous teenager.

Tuesday and Wednesday are the faceless twins that sit mutely midweek. They hang out together, loiter, and hope someone will take notice of them. They're steady and slow. Sometimes Wednesday gets the great nod by being referred to as "Hump Day."

How would it feel to be called Hump Day? The day between this and that, here and there. The day between weekends. This is why Wednesday is a faceless blockhead. He's always passed over for what came before and what is eagerly awaited. Wednesday is too dim-witted to know that the moniker Hump Day is just another way for people to say they're standing on him, overlooking him. He likes the nickname. It makes him feel included.

Tuesday, his sister, sits in his shadow. The wallflower of the week. She is sad, waifish, and has lank, greasy hair. She is malnourished and afraid to look you in the face. Tuesday is the day to get the oil changed, make plans, wait for them to happen, and get it over with—whatever "it" might be. It's possible that Tuesday has spent some time in the asylum. It's hard to live without love.

Thursday is the day next to Friday. She is the silent star of the week. She knows what she's about. She's smart, savvy and always true to herself. Sure, she's overlooked by the masses. But those in-the-know? They pay attention to Thursday. She's the one to watch, the day that carries the hope of the week. To understand this you have to look at Friday.

Friday is the know-it-all. He's the Man. He's everyone's best friend. The life of the party. The funny guy. He's the man of the hour. The one who has admirers hanging on him in bunches like overly ripe fruit. He's tall and good-looking. Commands attention. As it happens, he's also extremely vain and completely misinformed. In his bloated ego, he thinks he's the most important day of the week. Fat head. What does he know?

Thursday smiles to herself. She knows where the real power lies. It lies in hope. Thursday is the fulcrum of the week. She holds the might-have-beens, missed appointments and opportunities, lost hairbrushes and flat tires in her left hand. All the things her three younger siblings, Monday, Tuesday and Wednesday weren't able to grasp. In her right hand, she deftly wields the possibility of Friday, Saturday and Sunday while quietly overlooking Friday's narcissism. Overlooking shortcomings is one of Thursday's strengths.

Saturday and Sunday are the old married couple that everyone adores. Everyone wants to be just like them. They age gracefully, flawlessly and people wonder what the secret to their fabulous relationship is. In their old age, Saturday is grandma's pie, cookies, or rugelach. Sunday is Grandpa's funny stories, pipe smoke, lovable dodderingness. They always invite visitors in and make them completely at ease. Saturday and Sunday are all about comfort. They don't bully Monday, that's all his own misconception—where the cycle all begins.

Elephants

humidifiers
are thirsty elephants here
in the museum

THREE WEEKS AGO, I started a new job as a conservation lab assistant at a not-yet-open-to-the-public museum. One of my duties each morning and afternoon is to fill the three large humidifiers that occupy the storage area. These are needed to regulate the relative humidity in the huge warehouse space. It's typical for museums to attempt to keep the relative humidity at a constant level to help maintain the longevity of the collection. This is usually done by a museum-wide environmental control system. But since this is a new museum whose building is still under construction, I find myself filling the three humidifiers in the interim storage area twice a day. By day two of my new job I began calling it "Waltz of the Drunken Baby Elephants."

Each baby elephant is a big box that measures roughly three feet across, four feet long, and a little over three feet in height, with vents covering each of the long sides for the air intake and outflow. They are encased in a skin of almond-colored, powder-coated metal. Added to one of the short sides is a gray electrical box that controls the humidistat; this I dub the head. Opposite the head side is, well, that's where the water hose I use for filling the elephants is located. Logically, this would be the mouth, I suppose. But I've come to think of it as rather the opposite of the mouth and the source of my troubles ... at least, some of them.

The other source of my woes is the elephant's feet: Four sturdy casters, each of which has a mind of its own. These feet are the cause of the drunkenness. The elephant's belly holds up to thirty gallons of water. Imagine the most wily of shopping carts you may have encountered loaded with two-hundred and forty pounds of groceries. Now imagine navigating that unwieldy cart down an aisle crowded with priceless museum objects and you have an idea what it's like to waltz with drunken baby elephants. The only trouble with this comparison is that groceries are not generally given to sloshing. Water, however, is.

Last week I discovered something new. I was returning a very full Ned back from the watering station to his stall from having been watered when he seemed to want to turn around. Instead of struggling against him, I allowed him to back into his stall. It was thrilling to find that there were no accidents with this performance! His "stall" is a location in the southeastern corner of the warehouse near one of the two dock doors. Because of his location, near the large doors that lead outdoors and the frequent deliveries through those doors, Ned is one of the thirstiest elephants in my charge.

Ned is known as Humidifier #2 to everyone else on staff but me. The name Ned came to me one day as I labored to pass through the increasingly narrow aisles of the warehouse. Ned, in my mind, is the name of a weasel-faced banker, in a cheap, poorly fitted suit, whose eyes are beady and too close-set. His thinning hair should have been close-cropped years ago. Instead it hangs on, limply combed over the top of his shiny pate in a vague attempt to hide it. When the wind blows, the ruse is up. If Ned had been married, his wife would have told him to cut his hair. It's not astonishing to note that he has neither married nor cut his hair. His mannerisms are contrary to the flow of the natural world—Ned is out of synch with everything and everyone. In short, Ned is exasperating. This is how I came to name Humidifier #2.

The usual routine, until last Friday, is for Ned to leave numerous messes along the aisles as we clumsily dance through the warehouse. By the time we've gotten to his stall, I've used several paper towels to clean up his mess. The biggest mess comes when our turn around the dance floor is concluding. The water he's consumed burbles first from this side, then from that side in a hugely watery mess. I water Ned first so I can get it over with and finish on a happy note rather than a wet one.

Next is Dora. (Insert a happy sigh here.) Dora is the sweetheart. She is sure-footed and graceful, kindly, but not too bright. Were she a person, Dora might enjoy passing the time piecing together large jigsaw puzzles depicting exotic places she lacks the aplomb to visit. She would love to bring new neighbors in her apartment building tins filled with cookies and fudge. After all, she is a fantastic baker. Her secret desire in life is to be a dancer, though she lacks the physique for such an endeavor. Nevertheless, Dora is loveable. She maneuvers easily and when I return her to her stall she charmingly pirouettes into place. I have never once had to clean up after Dora. It is for this reason I christen her Dora the Darling.

Hap is taller and thinner than either Dora or Ned. Where Dora likes to be cooperative and Ned can't conceive of being anything but difficult, Hap just is. Like a Zen monk sitting in zazen, Hap is unflappable, focused and calm. If he had hands, they would be steady and quick to create. Were it not for one tiny problem, Hap might be my favorite. The snag in watering Hap is not due to any character trait at all. Sadly, Hap has the misfortune to be incontinent.

At first I thought I hadn't tightened the coupling that links Hap to the watering hose. But after a few warnings by my boss that one of my baby elephants was "piddling," I was sure something was amiss. It turns out Hap's coupling will unscrew itself if certain conditions exist, though I didn't figure this out until The Big Spill of My Third Week.

I had gotten dressed up that day: skirt, wide belt, kitten-heeled pumps, the whole nine yards. As one might imagine, this is not the best getup for dancing with the drunken baby elephants. But the man who had funded our entire museum thus far was making a big visit and I wanted to impress. As it happened, he asked me where I was from and, not being sure whether he was asking where I was from as in born or where I was from as in work experience, I dumbly bumbled through my answer—not one of my more articulate days. Luckily, my boss cut in to extol some of my more impressive resume elements.

He departed. I deflated. Suddenly my shoes were too tight, my hair too frumpy and the wide belt that had seemed smart that morning was now ridiculous.

It was in this frame of mind that I approached the final dance of the day. I wheeled Hap to the watering station, attached the hose, set my alarm to come back in ten minutes and walked away. I always set the timer and return to whatever I was working on previously. I abhor wasting time. Besides, listening to the elephant's belly fill is tantamount to watching paint dry. Off I went, back to the zither in desperate need of cleaning. I returned ten minutes later to The Big Spill.

When Hap had piddled in the past, it was a small amount, a watery sock under the coupling. This was Lake Champlain. I quickly shut off the water, unhooked the hose and began my laughably earnest attempt to clean up the spill using paper towels. Not wanting to panic or attract any attention to the sea that had spread under Hap, two large crates and a shelving unit four feet away, I nimbly assessed that I needed something larger and infinitely more absorbent. I recalled seeing the woman who came to clean with a large mop in a wheeled yellow bucket. Regrettably, she arrived about the same time of day that I water the baby elephants. All the same, I ran to the closet where I hoped it was kept, breathed a sigh of relief that could have been heard a block away, and stealthily deployed my new recruit to the spill site.

By now, my adrenaline had kicked in. It's nice and humid in the storage area, which in this instance made me perspire. The wide belt came off, as did the pointy shoes; neither was particularly helpful to getting down on my hands and knees to ascertain where the mop needed to go most quickly. The pencil skirt couldn't be helped. I swabbed and sweated. When I was finished, I furtively darted back to the maintenance closet. I hated to be caught yellow-bucketed, barefooted, loose-bloused, toting a mop. Grateful that most everyone departs right at five p.m., I slipped back into the storage area to don my shoes and belt. I paused for a moment to attempt smoothing the frizzy hair-wreck on top of my head and went to face my boss.

"Are the elephants watered?" My boss had picked up on my joke about the elephants.

"Mm-hmm." I nodded with a smirk and pursed lips. "Had a little trouble with that one that likes to piddle again." I chuckled convincingly, like I wasn't the least bit alarmed a few minutes ago about Lake Champlain.

"Lalee, you seem to be having a lot of trouble with those. Do we need to get you a kiddie pool?"

"Kiddie pool," I laughed a little harder. I had to leave soon or my laughter would become some kind of uncontrollable fit. "That's a good one. Yes! That is EXACTLY what I need."

I laughed even more and made a hasty exit past her to grab my things and leave for the day.

Two weeks later, Hap did it again. This time however, I was prepared. I don't have a kiddie pool, but I do have a plastic bin that I've used under Ned, Dora and Hap since that day. Of course, I've only needed it for Hap. After one month and one Big Spill I feel I've successfully mastered the Waltz of the Drunken Baby Elephants.

È Petaloso

yellow confetti
jettisoned by green-barked trees
è petaloso

THE MOMENT I HEARD IT my heart opened wide, as inwardly I traveled to Italy. There I met Matteo, an eight-year-old schoolboy, who had penned the non-word "petaloso" in his assignment to list adjectives that describe flowers.

"How clever you are! I love words too. Thank you for creating this one. Did you know Italian is my favorite language? È la più bella lengua nel mundo.[1]"

Petaloso is a combination of the Italian *petalo* for petal and the suffix *–oso* or "full of" creating a word for "full of petals." How lovely and creative and perfectly spring.

··· • ···

IN THE DARKNESS of predawn, I woke thinking about Thursday, haiku and the what-will-it-be that happens when I don't have something bubbling on the back burner. A giant, green-barked palo verde tree I'd seen daily came to mind. Under it, a yellow drift of discarded blossoms. Cherished by the tree, courted by the wind, admired by me.

A small nudge to grab the pocket-sized journal I keep in my purse came to me. My mind wanted to just write the "yellow confetti" in my regular journal, but something else urged me again to grab the tiny booklet. I opened it to the first blank page, and there next to it was:

petaloso
è molto bene![2]

I was instantly reminded of Matteo's story, which I'd heard on NPR during my drive to work earlier this month. It was just what I needed to complete this haiku. I hope wherever you are, your spring is *molto petaloso.*[3]

1. It is the most beautiful language in the world.
2. Is great! (In the writer's poor Italian, not literal.)
3. Very full of petals.

Word Crow

gathered "confuzzled"
a silly fabrication
shiny, word-crow find

MEL USED THE WORD "confuzzled" to describe how he felt about something. I found it a terribly clever and funny conglomeration of confused and puzzled, tucking it away for future use.

I work with Mel at the auto auction, he's one of my bosses. My gathering of "confuzzled" coincided with several of my coworkers chiding me for using "big words." It happened often enough that inwardly I began to cringe when someone else would repeat the offending word. ("Vernacular?") I was embarrassed they had noticed my word choice and was reminded of middle school, where the moniker "brain" was unkindly used in reference to me.

Even if the ornithologists at Cornell prove otherwise, the myth that crows enjoy finding and keeping shiny objects persists. This image of a crow came to me while journaling about the somewhat painful experience of coworkers noticing my vocabulary.

The truth is, I've always loved words. When I was a very small child, I would often be lulled to sleep by images of detailed and overlapping words swimming in my inner vision. These images were accompanied by a pleasant and unusual feeling of floating movement, all of which arrived moments before I would be carried off to my dreams.

Treasuring words is so much a part of me that I hadn't really noticed it until this past week when Mel's silly word corresponded with curious looks and remarks regarding my word choices. I am grateful for this experience—turning something uncomfortable into an opportunity for me to appreciate a previously overlooked part of myself.

Borborygmus

real borborygmus
belly rumbler of a word
you can look it up

I WASN'T SURE I could trust the dusty childhood memory. I tried looking up the word I remembered my brother saying when we were growing up. I remembered it as "borderigmy," which certainly sounds like a totally made-up word. My brother would most often use it at the dinner table or after a meal and would pat his belly saying, "Mmm … borderigmy …" in a funny voice and laugh, which would make me laugh.

The vague and random memory came to me a couple of years ago. I tried all manner of spellings and still came up empty-handed. I had been thinking about what I call my inner word crow and how I'd been embracing it more and more. But, I had to relegate the word and the memory to a distant back burner, shrugging inwardly and conceding that I must have misremembered the events, or at the very least, my brother had made up a word with his friends.

··· • ···

A FEW WEEKS AGO, a trip to one of the first museums I'd ever worked in caused me to reflect on the training I'd received while trying to be a docent. (It didn't work out. I'm not really docent material—especially not when it comes to natural history. My talents, it turned out, lay elsewhere in the museum world). In any case, the only thing I remembered from my training was this: coprolite.

Yes indeedy. Hours of training and note taking and I took away the word for fossilized feces. Dinosaur dukey. Paleo poop. Calcified caca. A totally tough turd.

Shortly after the trip, I shared the word coprolite with my sister and mused I'd discovered a collection I could start that wouldn't take up space anywhere but in my head: I could collect words I found amusing.

When I shared this love of bizarre words with my sister (the Merriam-Webster Dictionary app for smart phones allows one to keep a list of beloved words. I love this about it!), we bantered back and forth about funny words. She knew widdershins but not syzygy.

As we were talking, she was also looking at her computer. Finally, she turned the screen around to reveal the word borborygmus. I read the definition: intestinal rumbling caused by moving gas.

"OHMYGOD! That's the word! That's the word I was looking for!" I shouted, "Jimmy used to say that! Do you remember that? I thought maybe I made the word up! Or

I'd fabricated another memory. I'm so excited!" I quickly plugged the word into my dictionary to hear how the word was pronounced. Bor-bor-IG-mus. The plural was borborigmi, pronounced with the last syllable sounding like "my" as in, "This is *my* new word."

Within the next few days, I shared the word with my bosses and they got a kick out of it. Who knew? A word for intestinal rumblings.

A few weeks later, my brother came to visit to celebrate my parents' sixtieth wedding anniversary. At some point while he was here, I mentioned the word. He repeated it as sounding like "borborigmee" AH! No wonder I thought the word from my memory sounded different. "Where on earth did you learn that word?" I asked.

From a George Carlin routine that he'd listened to, no doubt on a record, at a friend's house. He admitted it was something he probably shouldn't have been listening to as a kid, but there it was, the origin of the mystery word I'd been trying to find for a couple of years.

As a complete alpha/omega bookend experience, I told my bosses about where my brother had found the word. A few key taps on his smartphone later, one boss found the clip online and, with the door closed to our office, we listened to the whole skit. There it was, among other funny noises humans' bodies make, "borderigmy". Carlin himself mispronounced the pluralized version of the word (admitting he may be saying it wrong). And thus came to a close a vocabulary mystery solved after more than thirty years. Magical.

What started as a genuine interest to know something for the simple joy of learning taught me a deeper lesson: Despite hitting a roadblock in the beginning, unable to find the word at all, the glimmering desire to know the truth never went away. It hovered in my heart for years until, it seems to me, something larger than myself could line up all the pieces necessary to complete the learning process.

It ties into a phrase I got, several decades ago in contemplation when looking at a goal. It was five simple words: Patience and persistence of pursuit. The slow cadence of this story's unfoldment made it that much sweeter when it fully emerged. I wonder, what other long, slow story arcs are at work in my life that I may have forgotten about? Because now I believe, a genuine desire to know truth will never go unanswered.

Lemonade

recipe hunting
sugar but not saccharine
lemony balance

I HAD A SECOND-GRADE TEACHER who never stopped smiling. As a kid I thought this was kind of neat. Plus, it certainly beat the stern first-grade teacher I had who rarely smiled and didn't think much of me in comparison to my older brother whom she adored.

My mother described my teacher's propensity for prolonged grinning, by imitating her. Through clenched teeth and a false smile Mom would joke, "She wouldn't say the word 'shit' if she had a mouthful of it."

She also used the term "saccharine" to describe my teacher's demeanor. I inferred that it meant she was falsely sweet, because once my mom pointed it out, I realized my teacher really didn't seem happy or nice. It was a façade.

I was thinking of this grade-school teacher when I dusted off the term "saccharine" from among other musty memories of childhood. Not realizing the word I sought had an 'e' on the end, I typed "saccharin" into my favorite online dictionary. I was dismayed to find that saccharin is the name for the chemical concoction used as a fake sweetener.

How could my mom have used that term for my teacher? I was sure it meant something else, I wondered.

Persistence and curiosity paid off when I typed in "saccharine" to find the definition I'd had in mind. Both "cloyingly agreeable or ingratiating" and "exaggeratedly sweet or sentimental," matched what I was trying to convey.

What does this have to do with recipe hunting? As it happens, I'm not terribly good at making lemonade, either figuratively or literally. At least, that's how I was feeling when I wrote the haiku. I'd been seeking the perfect recipe to turn my struggles, with the hill of lemons I felt I'd been shuffling through for months and years, into refreshing lemonade. I wanted a way to bring the right amount of sugar—real, earthy cane sweetness—into my life to balance the sour citrus. I wanted it to be genuine though. Not cloying or sentimental or exaggerated, but the real sweetness that comes with true contentment.

The sweetness I've found comes from savoring the little things I love: A good cup of black coffee first thing in the morning, going for walks with my husband, watching the sun change the sky to crimson beauty from my kitchen window, my two cats sitting with me as I write in the mornings. That's the real sugar.

The lemons are still there. My new recipe just calls for more sugar than I was previously using.

Sonorisionary

seventy years pass
before full moon greets the sun
in solstice glory

WHILE PONDERING this week's haiku, I got sidetracked. But in a lovely, meandering way. Sidetracked sounds too edgy, hard and judgmental. My experience needed a rounded word. A spiral word that softens the heart but focuses the mind to Soul's purpose, not Ego's. It was such a lovely journey. Inspiring. Indeed, little side trips like this *are* inspiring. Sidetracked is the bumbling humpous word that Ego uses to inform us, hands on reprimanding hips, we've gone astray from whatever menial (and perhaps meaning*less*) trip we're focusing on.

As I typed that last sentence I mistyped "focusing" and instead typed "forcusing." Immediately, I thought, *HA! forced focusing = FORCUSING,* which runs along the same vein as sidetracked. Another ego-driven activity.

Let's propose some new words then, something different from sidetrack. Words to indicate when we've stepped onto the magical path where imagination and creation meet to walk off into the sunset. Only the film doesn't stop rolling there, we're allowed to tag along this enchanted path that lights up only in their presence.

> ***chariyoyo:*** Chariot and yoyo—it's fun. It gallops along and yet is kept in hand when it yoyos back, with a satisfying smack to our palm, and we grasp something new. Yes, perhaps chariyoyo is a candidate.
>
> EXAMPLE: I got chariyoyoed this morning while researching this year's solstice and happened across a wonderful website.

> ***meanderling:*** It has a cheery way about it—a certain sweetness and simplicity that connects us to the childlike wonder of Soul. If you've been meanderling you may have discovered something new in your worlds, or perhaps something ancient and deep, like hidden treasure gleaming in the recesses of your inner self.
>
> EXAMPLE: During this morning's meanderling, I found a book titled *Lost in Translation: An Illustrated Compendium of Untranslatable Words from Around the World.* And though I already know I love words, the discovery that a work like this exists sparked childlike delight and excitement that continues to ricochet around my imagination, motivating my creativity.

sonorisionary: Someone who heeds the call of their inner vision to bring back a gem of insight that may or may not pertain to the masses but adds to the collective raising of human consciousness nonetheless.

EXAMPLE: Focusing (not forcusing) on something we love is in itself a sonorisionary act. Whether we share that love outwardly in recognizable forms or not, it emanates from us like ripples on the water. And that in turn, seen or unseen, adds to the world around us.

The sonorisionary is someone who knows how to master the meanderling, who cherishes the chariyoyo. We all do it when we are focusing on something we love. Where does your meanderling take you? When was the last time you were chariyoyoed? Remember, you ARE the sonorisionary.

CREATIVE WRIT

Inspiration Arrives

inspiration drives
a '63 Impala
arrives unannounced

A RECENT TRIP TO THE THEATRE, to see a spectacular one-man-show called *A Weekend with Picasso*, reminded me of a fantastic quote by the famous artist:

"Inspiration exists, but it has to find us working."

As I sat down at the computer to write, or at least try, because the last few weeks had been a struggle of jumbled, lost, weed-wacked words, Picasso's own words got me to imagining …

··· • ···

INSPIRATION DRIVES a 1963 Chevy Impala. It's lowered or "bagged" one might say. In some neighborhoods, this makes ridiculous busybodies nervous if they happen to glance out of the window and spy her gliding past. The Impala is impeccably maintained and whisper quiet. Inspiration's not looking for a drag race, but a comfortable ride. She is cool.

Ultimately hip, there's absolutely no denying that. Everyone is in agreement on this fact.

She does not stand on ceremony or any Victorian frippery like calling cards. In fact, if you're answering the door for someone, it's definitely not Inspiration. This is how she finds you:

Hers is a 24/7/365 kind of job. She cruises incessantly. She is everywhere at once, omniscient and omnipresent, wandering the streets, waiting to see who is ready to receive her. Are the lights on? Is someone home? Is the garden tended? Plants healthy? Weeds to a minimum? Has the inhabitant been taking all the steps she can on her own?

Inspiration must find you working. She can hone in on the vibration of creation. Wherever you are, if you're working on your craft, be it writing, painting, sculpting, composing, baking, woodworking, whatever your craft is, she will find you. This is how she found me:

She arrived unannounced on a Monday morning. I peeked out the window and saw her car, I was in my PJs and hadn't had enough coffee yet, but I opened the door to find nothing there.

The next morning, I was persistent, she was persistent, and when she arrived, on a Tuesday, she found me, seated in the blue armchair, sporting my pink fuzzy robe, messy hair, legs crossed under me to support my laptop and pouring out words as they came. Sense or no sense. Good words or lame.

Inspiration found me writing—it was her invitation. She had slipped off her combat boots without effort and padded in sock feet to the living room where I was working. I paused in my tapping and with coffee breath offered her a mug of the same. She accepted with a warm smile. I noticed her hair was a bit messy too. I felt less self-conscious.

What is left in the room once she's departed? Is it a sad thing? Oh no. No it's not. The room is full of electric possibility. Of round vowels and savvy consonants—the shapes of the unformed, and the air is fresh with rain, or is it just-baked bread? No matter. It fills you with energy and drive, and it oozes out of your pores as you write, paint, sculpt, compose, do *your* thing.

Eventually, the good stuff WILL come through, because Inspiration has found you at the stone or the computer or the canvas, and what you thought you would do is not what it ends up being, but that doesn't matter because the act of just doing it is what invites the almighty Inspiration in.

Blank Page

vacuous white page
stares, glares, and insinuates
incompetency

A T LEAST A BLANK STARE is innocuous. Fairly harmless.
It generally says more about the person wearing it than
the person on the receiving end. Generally.

But a blank page? Oh that's a look filled with venom. It
speaks volumes about the writer facing it. Blank white rat
bastard.

Writing is so much easier if you actually feel you have
something to say.

I usually try to leave myself a hint. A whiff of a plan when
I stop my writing practice for the day. And if I don't write
for a day? I'm a little slow the next day.

Two days away from the writing? I limp to the computer.

Three days or more? I'm nearly catatonic with the brain's
equivalent of constipation.

Where is the brain bran?

How to get going again?

This haiku was written on one of those nights when I felt I couldn't possibly think of anything to say—and when I looked to the blank page for encouragement, insight and/ or inspiration—well that's when I got the above.

Ironically, it served to remind me that there is power in the discipline. Showing up is half the battle. Being willing to take a turn or two around the dance floor with some clunky phrases wearing wooden clogs is all part of it.

Can't knock it out of the ballpark every time, I remind myself.

The last few days, the blank spots in the calendar where I track my word count? They feel the same as the big open blank white page armed with the frigid vastness of the tundra at high noon in midwinter shouting into the snow-blind white:

INCOMPETENCY!
IMPOSTER!

Sometimes coaxing out the ideas is like trying to catch feral cats. It's dangerous, they're fast, and they can shred the hell out of you with their claws.

White page, with a stare that insinuates I'm incompetent. Yessirree. There is nothing like a big ol' case of writer's block. Nothing like writing a bunch of drivel to make you feel like an idiot for trying.

Yep. The Blank Page and the Inner Critic? They're in cahoots. Two cheese monkeys sharing cheap, shitty beers and stale pretzels in a dive bar at the intersection of Subconscious and Self-Esteem where the streetlight flickers on-off, on-off, on-off in a Morse-code SOS headed Uptown.

What a gig those two jokers have going …

Obstinate Crabs

sometimes words don't come
skittering sideways like crabs
but squat obstinate

THIS IS THE SECOND in a two-part series about writer's block, blank pages, and the harsh inner critic we all face whether we're writing or not. When we left off last time, here's where we were:

The cheese monkeys Blank Page and the Inner Critic were discovered to be in cahoots, sharing cheap, shitty beers and stale pretzels in the dive bar at the intersection of Subconscious and Self-Esteem.

··· • ···

BLANK PAGE SHOWS UP FIRST. Always. He grabs a seat at the end of the bar. No matter how big a man Inner Critic thinks he is, he's always second fiddle to Blank Page. Why? Because Blank Page shows up first and makes a power play of it. He picks the seats; Inner Critic has to follow his lead.

And follow he does.

Blank Page will have had at least one beer by the time Inner Critic shows up. Then he sits and kibitzes with the bartender, an unwitting accomplice in this charade. A short, no-necked hack, the bartender serves up weak metaphors and overused phrases like pouring a lukewarm beer. Kinda flat, kinda bitter. Nothing good comes of the time these three spend together.

If Blank Page has the power in the beginning, by the end of the evening, he's too blotto to hold a decent conversation (which in truth, he sucks at anyway), and Inner Critic has unleashed his vim and vitriol upon Blank Page and our squat, no-neck Bar Tender whom we've yet to give a name. It's really pretty pathetic.

Outside, the flickering SOS streetlamp puts itself to sleep, no help having arrived in the swift form of inspiration.

Our no-neck, squat bartender shoos the incapacitated duo out the door and, with a hammy-hand, turns the lock behind them.

Blank Page schlumps a half-block down Subconscious before turning into an alley and falling gracelessly behind a dumpster, after having heaved his final beer in a resounding splat.

Inner Critic, slyly kept most of his wits about him (he didn't drink as much as Blank Page), fairly skips a few blocks down Self-Esteem, where the neighborhood is being gentrified, and lets himself into an immaculately well-kept, if uninspired, brownstone that's been in his family for generations.

He sits down at his own typewriter, carefully pulls a

piece of paper from the sheaf in the lower right desk drawer, rolls it into position, places his hands above the keyboard and waits. It only takes a moment for the connection and he's off, his fingers typing as fast as the manual typewriter allows. He's got a cadence to it so that the keys don't bind up into a tangled mass.

It pours forth almost endlessly. A litany of coarse cut-downs and belittling drivel. He repeats himself, but that doesn't matter. He just needs to keep going. To keep convincing the person on the other end of the paper, the reader, who is also today's writer, that the effort is pointless. No good can come from writing. Why bother?

He continues tapping into the wee hours of the morning until he makes one final, emphatic gesture on the keyboard and halts his composing. He yawns, laces his fingers together making a show of stretching his arms above his head, pulls the paper from the carriage, crumples it into a ball and throws it into a wire trash basket where it joins dozens of its bretheren.

Inner Critic yawns again and casually takes the cover he'd forgotten to make use of last night (which is odd for him, he's usually so meticulous!), placing it carefully on the typewriter. He bends to touch his toes as he stands, then takes the waste basket into the kitchen where he dumps it into a larger trash can, reminding himself to take that out on the morrow, for trash pickup is the day after.

He returns the wire basket deskside and heads up the stairs to his bedroom, passing the closed doors to guest rooms on the way. They've never been used. Nevertheless, he has the housekeeper change the linens regularly so they're fresh and inspects the rooms from time to time to make sure they're kept clean. He's sure someday someone will want to stay. Possibly even Blank Page. One never knows. It could happen.

DAJIBAN!

Dajiban racing
an ungainly elegance
that speaks of passion

A WIDE AND UNSTOPPABLE GRIN spread across my face. It stayed for not only the duration of the video I was watching, but for the rest of the day. And whenever I think about this video I smile.

DAJIBAN!

What is this word? It is a word for passion, or at least one sort of passion. A quite specific one actually: The Japanese passion for racing Dodge vans. Mm-hm. Racing. Dodge. Vans.

It's pretty spectacular.

Watching the video (courtesy of my awesome bosses) is to catch the coattail of something wonderful. It might not be your idea of wonderful. I can tell you it certainly wasn't mine. And yet, there it is, passion, in living, breathing, V8-powered, gorgeous, human color.

••• • •••

When I interned at the conservation lab at the Smithsonian's Natural History Museum in my final year of grad school, I was sent to help process artifacts in the Archaeology Department for a week. That's fancy wording for bagging rocks. At least, that was my impression after the first day.

But then something magical happened. The guy I was working for started to talk about these rocks I was bagging. His entire countenance changed and he lit up as he talked about the lithics, and what he could see and read in the rock. Each had a story, and he cherished each one of those stories. Through his love of lithics a whole world opened up to me. It wasn't my world or even a world I wanted to hang out in really, but there was something utterly compelling about this guy's enthusiasm for rocks.

It is really uplifting to be in the presence of someone who loves what they're doing. Uplifting seems too paltry, I'd go so far as to say transcendent. Not only that, but it's infectious. Every time I have basked in the presence of someone who loves something, however quirky that thing might seem, I walk away more resolute to follow my own passion.

It was a number of years after grad school, midway through my museum career, that I met The Washing Machine Man of Colorado. (His real name is Lee Maxwell.) I'd heard about him from another colleague. His collection was open to the public but only by appointment. I scheduled a time for a small group of museum professionals to visit.

I had preconceived ideas. I admit it. I expected some grungy dust-covered collection in a dingy barn with a heavy air of half-finished thoughts and meandering oddity that accompanies someone who is not only muttering to himself but, well, a bit crazy. I mean, who in his right mind collects washing machines?

Next to a very tidy turn-of-the-last-century house, were two prefab metal buildings, inside of which were housed his vast collection. It progressed logically from washboards and wringers, to more modern and identifiable machines. The earlier models are the ones he had so lovingly restored in a workshop that held the calm, sacred beauty of any sanctuary. It was inspiring to be among all these things he had worked on—for that attention is a form of love. And to visit, is to bask in that bright, cared-for energy.

Yes. It seems kooky. But there was an ineffable quality to being in the presence of that focused attention.

It was magnificent.

··· • ···

WHEN I WATCHED the *DAJIBAN!* (I just have to say it with an exclamation point! And *italicized ALL CAPS* in an attempt to capture, in printed word, the feeling of acceleration and excitement.) video, I was reminded of The Washing Machine Man and the Lithics Guy, and it made me want to grab the world by its shoulders and shout, "See? There IS great beauty in this crazy world! Go out there and find your quirky thing!

Dive in! Get excited! Be a little kooky! In doing so, you might just inspire someone else."

Go forth and *DAJIBAN!*

*"Willpower will always take second chair
to the imagination."*

—Harold Klemp, *Journey of Soul*

Willpower vs. Imagination

an epic battle
rigid willpower versus
imagination

WILLPOWER FURIOUSLY FIDDLED, overreaching, attempting to overachieve, anxious, fidgety and grossly under-experienced (despite his great age). He wildly thrashed his bow across the violin strings to screech out an entirely disharmonious tune—best efforts and all. This was his moment. He finally had the limelight. And what light it was! His best light, he was certain.

Eyes clenched closed, creating a Neanderthal-worthy unibrow, sweat poured from his high forehead (some might call this a receding hairline), all elbows and knees, angles and points. He was in the moment, of the moment, poised on the edge of the eternity of his thoughts. Bliss.

His final note echoed, a hairline crack from nails on a chalkboard, and wandered off to silence. Opening his eyes, he rested bow and violin on opposite knees and smiled, cozy with the warmth of his insular smugness. Clearly, this time he'd win the competition for first chair.

As he marched off stage, back rigid with imperious certitude, he was passed by Imagination, swathed in a colorful cape of swirling light, seeming to float, just above the stage. *Why that buffoon doesn't even have a violin in hand!* Willpower mused with a sneer.

Imagination paused, allowing the swirling cape to come to a dazzling rest just as she stretched her leg to daintily extend a pointed toe. A delicate, singular flute note sounded. Then Imagination began to dance in earnest. Each movement, emboldened by an invisible inner strength, created its own sound. Woody, sweet oboes were joined by deep bassoon, cello, bass and violins with a crescendo of bold brass.

An orchestra of celestial sound swept over the concert hall, filling it so that even the walls themselves felt they could no longer contain such beauty. Their very molecules changed by the exuberant energy emitted with Imagination's movement made them want to burst with joy.

Just as the walls thought they could expand no further, the symphony came to a sweet end as Imagination tiptoed back to center stage, flushed from the effort, or humbly blushing, or both. She'd done her best, and that was enough. She bowed her head briefly and exited the stage with a broad smile and small, shy wave.

UNEMPLOYMENT = OPPORTUNITY

Unemployment = Opportunity

smug interviewer,
so where do you see YOURself
in five freakin' years??

TODAY I'M ANGRY.

I'm angry with the smug, solidly fifty-something man who interviewed me and asked in closing, with a mocking grin, "Where do you see yourself in five years?"

I made a face.

"Three years. Where do you see yourself in three years?" He amended.

"Who still asks that question?" Is what I might have countered, what I wish I'd had the moxie and agility of intellect in the moment to do.

But, really. Who still asks that question?

There was a time when I confidently replied, "In your job." And I meant it. I really had.

Fourteen years ago, they asked, "Where do you see yourself in ten years?" Because fourteen years ago, ten years

73

was the go-to number asked out of a sense of security and comfort created in the previous decade.

It's telling that it's down to five years. And even so? So much can change in five years …

What I'd like to tell this interviewer, is that I haven't had a framework for my life since 2008 when I was laid off from my last "real" job. The last job that felt like success. That looked like something I wasn't embarrassed to say I did for a living. The last job that didn't make me feel desperate to find something else. The last time I felt like an adult with direction.

And yes. Sometimes I feel quite adrift and hopeless without that framework.

But what has taken the place of that sturdy security?

I've created a steely alliance with change. Any thought I had that I was "secure" has been washed away. My new best friend and confidant? Change. I can count on Change. Security was the popular, attractive person I thought I wanted as a best friend. But Change? Change is who I hang with now. We don't have a real plan for where we're headed. I mean, we make plans, Change and I, but then, well, you never know. Sometimes they come to fruition, sometimes they don't. It's all good.

Change is the kind of friend I'm slightly embarrassed to introduce to my friends and family. Like most people, they too like the clean-cut looks of Security. Who doesn't like good looks? But Change has their own beauty—once you get past the messy mop of hair and beat-up leather jacket.

74

They're not derelict or anything. They don't smell bad and aren't unclean. They brush and floss regularly. They just don't always present well, but that's all on the surface.

I've learned a lot from Change. Their command of resilience and flexibility has taught me a thing or two about those qualities. Sure, I haven't mastered them. But now they're a part of my daily, go-to toolbox. And that has made all the difference. By embracing Change in a warm bear hug at every turn (or even trying to) I've taken steps into a more expansive state of contentment.

··· • ···

I WROTE THAT HAIKU in the spring of 2014 and I'd been unemployed for eight months. In month three without work, as I was standing in the vet's office receiving news that our Maine Coon, my fur baby Bashad was terminally ill, my husband called to say he'd just been laid off.

I tried not to panic.

But I must have looked decidedly panicked; when I stepped back into the vet's office they asked if I needed to sit down.

I drove home thinking, *This is where the rubber meets the road. This is where I get to practice detachment and trust. This is where I get to adopt a different attitude from the last time I was unemployed.*

I sat down the next morning to do some calculations. I tallied up the first ninety-six months (eight years) of our marriage to conclude my husband and I had both been employed full time twenty-six of those months. Sometimes he had a full-time job, sometimes I did. Throughout those other seventy months, there were varied permutations of full- or part-time work by one or both of us.

Here I'll interject that at the time of this writing, in October 2020, I have a full-time job, but my husband, like millions of others due to the pandemic, is out of work. My job is not permanent and may end with the fiscal year, in June 2021.

I have to ask, why so much unemployment? Why the struggle?

Among the clutter of dusty fears and musty unknowns, something glitters: It's the knowledge that, however long a stretch of unemployment lasts, an opportunity will present itself. It always has—albeit pretty much never on the timeline I'd hoped for. And that's one of the gems I've gleaned from our numerous encounters cozying up to unemployment, with its rollercoaster ride of highs (I got an interview!) and lows (They hired someone else. How are we going to pay for X, Y, Z?)

I answer the questions briefly to conclude: these experiences brought me insight and hard-won wisdom in a way I wouldn't have been able to via other means—unemployment brings opportunities.

A Curator

guarding my pleasures
curating my contentment
good morning coffee

I LOVE COFFEE. It is the taste of my parent's home in Scottsdale. It is cribbage and Scrabble and time spent together. It is black-and-white German kitchens with accents of red. It is every café visited from Berlin to Brindisi, Assisi to Mont Saint-Michel, San Francisco to Fort Lauderdale. It is coffee-shop dates with my husband, late night dancing, and every morning I sit cross-legged, pen poised above my journal. Coffee is one of my greatest pleasures.

Lately, guarding my pleasures has started to feel like the ultimate experience in gratitude. I have only just become aware of this experience while drinking my cup of coffee in the morning. In that first sip, I am at once totally present and awash with memories that remind me of great love. It is so simple, yet brings me such joy. I wonder where else might I find such simple pleasures. And when I find them, I will guard them by being fully present and grateful for them.

Seeking out these little clues is one of the ways I'm learning to curate my own contentment, to take responsibility for my life and happiness in a way I don't know that I often have—or perhaps ever have. But I do it with coffee and I have for decades. Ask anyone who has ever traveled with me, "What's the first thing she does when exploring a new city?"

The answer will inevitably be, "Find the coffee." They may argue it's because I need it to wake up. That is partially true. But only because it is with my pen, and journal, and coffee that I awaken my creativity, call forth a connection with Soul, and explore the links between my inner and outer lives every morning. I guard this pleasure.

I wonder too, by allowing something so small to take on such giant proportions of pleasure and contentment, will that intention and attention help to diminish those other, larger, more scary aspects of my life? I think it's an experiment worth conducting.

As a museum professional, I have curated many different kinds of collections in my career. I know how to preserve them, guard them against the agents of deterioration. Being unemployed is offering me a new opportunity to find those agents at work deteriorating my own contentment, to cull my collection as it were, and guard those pleasures that bring me gratitude.

Surrender

admitting defeat
is maybe like surrender
only one has grace?

CURIOUSLY, AND IN AN INTERESTING TWIST of serendipity (perhaps even irony?), the word of the day on my Merriam-Webster® dictionary app is *aplomb*, which they define as complete and confident composure or self-assurance: poise.

Ha! Aplomb is perhaps the exact opposite of what I feel today.

A few days ago, I came across a book I'd read for a book club five or six years ago. In the back I'd written down gems I'd pulled from the reading. The one that stood out to me most was this:

grace = expecting the best and accepting what comes

As I journaled this morning, I looked at our current situation: what might be called the space between a rock and a hard place. I wrote:

"... we can surrender (admit defeat) and ..."

insert the rock, or the hard place either one, as both are

completely undesirable, and neither seem to be what I would conceive of as the "best" but rather "what comes" and must be accepted.

This got me thinking about the two words I'd penned: defeat and surrender. Aside from the white flag, what IS the difference?

Defeat feels to me as if I go down, fallen, with a loud and resounding painful thump. Crushed under the weight of my own armor perhaps. Clutching in one hand my expectations, the other twitching to grasp at something just out of reach.

Surrender has much more serenity. Maybe it saw some battle action, maybe not. Maybe the gauze it used to bandage the wounds from drubbings was cleverly used to sew the white flag. Surrender is at least standing, if not with total aplomb perhaps.

Defeat has to haul itself up, armor creaking, dented, dirty and stinking of failure. Surrender stands at the ready, makeshift white flag waving in the wind of change that brought it to this place, and steps toward the future, the eternal now.

Sotto Voce

quiet yet mighty
soul's sotto voce guides us
mundane to sublime

INTUITION. SIXTH SENSE. NUDGE. We all have a unique inner voice. This, I am convinced, is Soul's sotto voce. In the crowded and often overwhelmingly noisy cocktail party of life, Soul hovers at our elbow, waiting to whisper insight and direction directly in our ear. It is so quiet as to be nearly imperceptible. It is meant for us alone. No one else can hear this voice. And, it is up to us to hone our listening skills because, like the cocktail party, there are many competing voices and visions in our lives.

We've all heard Soul's whisper. "Turn right here."

And maybe we follow it or maybe our mind overrides it saying, "That's stupid. I never turn right here," as we sail past the right turn, headed for the other turn we are used to taking.

Or maybe it's not a voice but a nudge: Take down the model number of those eyeglasses.

And our mind butts in again, "Ugh. Please. They're glasses. It's not like they're going anywhere."

Yet when we return? The glasses (or shoes, or book, or, or, or. Insert your own story here), we wanted are gone. The sales person asks if we have the model number. Inwardly, I kick myself, (maybe we all do this, maybe it's peculiar to me), my mind, traitorously ready to switch sides with lighting ease declares, "What an idiot. I told you to write that number down!"

But it wasn't the mind. It was Soul.

Recently, I had an experience with this that makes me wonder, if I followed that voice as often as I could, would my life be more … sublime? More magical? Would I feel like I'm more in tune with life and the Universe? Because here's what happened:

I wasn't feeling well. I was feeling poorly enough that I begged out of going for a walk with a friend even though it was an amazing spring-like day. My head hurt and I had a general feeling of queasiness. I wanted to curl up on the couch with a book and nap. But I kept getting a really clear nudge to go to a specific shop to look for a necklace. I had been given a gorgeous, glass seahorse pendant, but had no way to wear it. I tried to ignore the nudge. But it was really strong.

Here is the thing about Soul's sotto voce: for me it often, in fact nearly always, defies reason and logic. Logically, I could list several reasons not to go to this store. I wasn't feeling well. I didn't need to spend the money. They might not have what I need. I was tired. Blah. Blah. Blah.

Yet, logic is of the mind and Soul doesn't care about its flimsy excuses. Soul is in-the-know and always has our best and highest good at heart. I am convinced of this because although I have been disappointed when I didn't follow a nudge or that quiet inner voice, I have never been disappointed when I have. I might add too, that sometimes when I didn't follow Soul's quiet direction, I later saw how following it would have been beneficial in a way that wasn't immediately obvious to me at the time. (Oh, how my mind likes the immediately obvious!)

I listened to the nudge and went to the store. It's a sweet little boutique in a neat neighborhood. It's one of my favorite places. The owner of the shop directed me to the necklaces and went back to her conversation with another woman, the only other person in the store.

It's not a big place and I couldn't help but overhear what they were talking about: Life, big changes, taking risks and trusting the Universe to provide what we need. I went up to the counter to check out and showed them the pendant and necklace I'd picked out to go with it. This spurred a continuation of the conversation they were having, prompting me to blurt out my recent plans to move across the country on nothing more than nudges and intuition. I felt a moment's sheepishness, which was quickly engulfed by their kindness and kinship.

I walked out of the boutique with far more than a

necklace. I walked out with a renewed sense of excitement about our move, that it was part of a larger plan, and that unseen, highly loving forces were at work in my life. And to *think*, I would have missed all that if I hadn't listened to Soul's sotto voce.

Paperbirds

paperbirds in flight
migration on changing winds
fluttering future

······

grounded paperbirds
in arrested migration
waiting for hatchlings

······

single paperbird
traveled on vision's hunches
finally nesting

I T'S TRUE, paperbirds is a made-up word. As separate words, paper birds didn't convey the same thing to me. It looked odd, and so I used paperbirds in the first of three haiku. By the time I wrote the second one, I knew there would eventually be a third. I had no way of knowing it would be five months from the second to the third and when I wrote the first I never imagined the outcome would be so long in coming.

The image of my resumes, when I sent them out into the world, as birds on changing winds came to me last August shortly before my two-year, grant-funded position at a big history museum came to an end. I had been sending out resumes in earnest since April, but the one I sent in August was filled with even more hope, knowing September first signaled looming unemployment. Each resume took on an avian life of its own—and so the paperbird was born.

By November, with all my paperbirds shot down over fields of rosy hope, I attempted to quell the panic jobless-ness had brought. The day after Thanksgiving, an insightful friend counseled me to relax. My worry and anxiety was probably doing more damage than good. The following day, I heeded her advice by indulging in my secret, guilty pleasure: watching home improvement shows. If we had had cable, I'd have been glued to HGTV. As it was, my available choice was PBS's *This Old House*.

The episode was one in a series about a house in Bedford, Massachusetts, which featured the restoration of the wood windows. They showed the workshop of a window restoration place. When I saw the work being done, my heart opened and I began to cry. I wanted to do that! I didn't know why, but I had to know more.

When my husband got home from work, I informed him I'd just sent my resume to a woman in Peabody trying to get a job learning window restoration. After correcting my pronunciation of Peabody ("It's Peabiddy, not PeaBODY."), he asked if I realized it was in Massachusetts, knowing I had a difficult time with long dark winters.

"Ha, ha, and yes." I replied glibly before pulling out my laptop to read him the missive I'd sent to the woman who owned the window business, along with my well-polished resume. It was a holiday weekend, so I didn't hope to hear back until the following week sometime—if at all. It was a total shot in the dark.

The next day, however, I got a cheery response encouraging me to try places in Colorado that did the same kind of work to see if I liked it. And, if ever I was in the area, to look her up and she'd give me the tour. Secretly, I was hoping she would offer me a job. That was a little far-fetched given the distance and my general lack of experience.

Over the next month, I contacted four places in Denver that did window restoration. One ignored me completely. The next said yes to an informational interview and never returned subsequent calls or emails. Another automatically assumed I was from her competition and would only speak to me after I sent two versions of my resume to "prove" my background and sincerity. After that, when we spoke, she heartily dissuaded me from entering the field. The fourth was gruff, angry and spent most of his time badmouthing the business owner who had defensively demanded my resumes.

After this series of experiences, I contacted the window place in Peabody again, asking for any guidance as to who might be a good fit for the experience I sought. Once again, she responded promptly and kindly, beginning with, "Good for you!" followed by lots of helpful insight. Nevertheless, by the end of January the windows of opportunity (pun intended) remained firmly closed.

It was at this point, I employed a technique I'd never had good luck with, but friends had experienced good results, so I tried it again. I picked a symbol to represent a pursue-this-dream answer from the Universe. The symbol had meaning to me and was unusual enough that I wouldn't easily run across it. I watched and waited.

And waited.

Then I gave up. My husband wasn't happy at his job and we both felt a change would do us good. With all the hope we could summon, we made the decision, symbol or no, to move to Massachusetts. Two days later we saw the symbol—twice in a three-hour span. Then again a week later. And again, a week after that.

With each encounter, the symbol took on more meaning. In the second sighting, the symbol was featured as the name of a ship in a movie. A friend pointed out ships indicated setting sail on a new adventure. The third time, it revealed itself in another film, one having to do with an elusive and desirable dream that the protagonist acquired in the end.

And so that is why at this writing, I am sitting in a coffee shop in Massachusetts with three weeks of employment at the window restoration place under my belt. All it took was the right paperbird to find an open window.

Epilogue

A few weeks after publishing this essay, my new boss, the owner of the window business, texted me a picture of The Symbol, asking if I thought we needed this painting for the shop. She was joking, of course, and she had no way of knowing she'd just sent me a picture of my symbol. But in that moment, I knew that not only had my paperbird found an open window, it was just the right window for me.

Automotive Confection

newly discovered
automotive confection
Nissan Figaro

I WAS A LITTLE DOWN that day. I had been unemployed for nine weeks and was adrift. Some weeks were good. Some were awful. Some were two parts good to two parts awful, and this was one of those weeks. A good friend had been visiting and I found myself sad she'd gone. I was reminded that two others were spending time together at a professional conference. A conference I might have gone to if I'd still been in that field, which I was not, by desire and design. Still. I was a little down. It had been a day of ill-timed attempts to achieve small goals. By the end of the day, when my husband came home from his gainful employment, I was ready to throw in the towel.

On our way to run the final errand of the day, we were waiting at a light behind a red and white 1955 T-bird that was running rich. Or really, it was running just as a 1955 car should. We were reminded that it was Wednesday night, and that it was possible, given the direction the guy was headed, that there might still be a car show at a nearby mall. Our errand had us driving a mere block from the car show. So on our way home, my husband, ever faithful to the automotive junkie in me, swung by before we headed to the pizza place on our way home. As I got out of the car I wondered what marvels we might see. There were the usuals: an Edsel, a Bel Air (of course), a '69 Mustang that showed up on a flatbed trailer.

I was headed towards a BMW Isetta 600, saying, "You don't see those every day," when It, The Discovery, drove into the parking lot.

I wasn't sure what it was. Two doors, snappy round headlights flanking a diminutive grille, warm beige color, funky white hubcaps, a rolldown-looking convertible top. It reminded me of Italy in the 1960s. Then I noticed the driver was in the right-hand seat. I was stumped. But I had to know! I left the Isetta and the dialogue about it with my husband, and went to talk to the mystery car's driver.

"Your lights are on." I interrupted the crusty dude the driver was talking to. (Car shows breed crusty dudes.) I walked around to get a better look at it. The interior was newer.

A kit car? I wondered, unsure how I felt about the interior.

The driver thanked me for the lights and said, "Take a close look. You are the reason this car was ever built."

Nice line, I thought, but aloud said, "It's lovely. What is it?"

"A Nissan Figaro."

"A what? I've never heard of that. How did you come by such a car?" *A Nissan? Really?* My inner voice countered. This didn't look like any Nissan I'd ever seen.

"Well, I was looking for a '32 Chevy." The owner replied.

Laughter erupted from me, "I'd say you missed your mark a bit with this." I gestured towards the small car, smiling like a kid. It was adorable. A saltwater taffy confection of toy-like parts and details. My husband joined us and we spent the next quarter-hour listening to the details of the 1989 Figaro and the story behind this particular one's purchase.

There were only 8,000 of them built in Japan, but they were so popular with women, Nissan added another 12,000 cars to production. Still, demand was high, so cars were sold on a lottery basis. They came in four colors, one for each of the seasons. This one was fall's color—Topaz Mist. The subtle warm sand and linen color combination lent a certain gravitas to the decidedly lighthearted design. It was like pearls worn with a white t-shirt, jeans and Converse high-tops.

Come to think of it, that's something I would wear. No wonder I loved it.

By the time we left, my dour mood had been lifted by that sweet little car.

To Volunteer

no job prospects yet
but I'll start volunteering
at the library

I STARTED VOLUNTEERING on a Friday morning. I felt like I clicked with the people right away. There is a slight chance I may have gotten overly emotional thanking the woman I worked for. I was trying to explain why it meant so much to me. How devastating it can be to one's self-confidence to not be working—to feel like one has something to offer others. I sort of teared up a tiny bit and I think I embarrassed her New England sensibilities. Ah well …

I love libraries. They are one of my favorite places in the whole wide world. I'm not entirely sure why. I loved going to the library as a kid. I loved the smell, and the cool hush of the thick-walled building. Even though I didn't play chess, I loved the chess set in the children's section. It was heavy wood with big, sculptural pieces, probably ten-inches high. The table was low and the stools had leather-slung seats. They too were carved wood to match the table and pieces.

The same thing happened the other day when I started volunteering at my local library—I fell in love. I came home and I was just so happy. Ever since I lost my job, I've been hanging out at the library writing and researching. I don't know why I didn't consider volunteering two months ago, except I think I was certain I'd get a job more quickly. That sounds familiar. It was the same way in Denver. It was only after four months of unsuccessful job hunting that I decided to volunteer at a local library there too.

Here is what's accomplished every Friday morning I volunteer:

1. Getting Out of the House

A major accomplishment while unemployed is the simple act of getting out of the house. I definitely achieve that when volunteering. It is so nice to have someplace to go. Knowing that someone is counting on me to be there makes it different from say, getting out of the house to go grocery shopping or take a yoga class.

2. Face Time

Another benefit is meeting and interacting with people. After a while (really not that long), the conversation with my cats becomes stale. And while I AM an introvert and I enjoy time alone, there IS such a thing as too much time alone. I'm still new to the area and haven't made many friends. So reaching out to help is one way to try and do that. Or at least assuage the loneliness.

3. Self-Confidence

When I work at the library, I have a sense of offering something and also accomplishing something. When I arrive, there is a big cart full of books to be shelved. When I leave, that big cart is empty. Presto! Instant gratification. And somehow, accomplishing something outside the house seems much more momentous and exciting than folding the upmpteenth t-shirt out of the hundredth load of laundry. Often, in job searching, there is a terrible feeling of uselessness. The weight of never knowing when the job hunt will end with employment is staggering—like concrete boots on one's self-esteem, and every resume sent is like jumping into the icy river. Volunteering to do something I enjoy reminds me I DO have something to offer others.

4. Expanding Horizons

Each week offers a new opportunity to see what is appealing to me. My first week there, I came across Stacy London's *The Truth About Style*. I was seized by the urge to read it. So I did. I never would have gone looking for that book, but in following the nudge to read it, I learned a few new things about myself, and how to cultivate self-confidence. This week, a book titled, *The Brain That Changes Itself* by Norman Doidge, M.D. stood out to me. Possibly because Stacy London talked about neuroplasticity and that's what this book is about. No matter, I love finding new topics to read about and am fascinated to see what I'm drawn to next.

5. Acting As-If

And finally, I'd be lying if I didn't say that by volunteering where I think I'd like to work, I'm hoping to increase my chances of getting a job. I think of it as enacting the as-if principal. I'm acting as if I have a job at a library (if not this library, then at another nearby one).

Who knows what other gifts volunteering may bring? For now, I'm thrilled with these.

Epilogue

The as-if principal worked. After a number of months volunteering, a part-time position opened up. The person I worked with at the library encouraged me to apply. I did and was overjoyed to join the amazing staff of the Topsfield Town Library.

Beyond the Target

Whoopsy! missed the mark
sometimes it's not the target
but what lies beyond

I MISSED THE MARK on this one. I was aiming for some-thing big, something clear, something very concrete. I launched my arrow and for months it was aloft, airborne and aimed at a very specific target. Yesterday, news of the arrow's landing reached me.

Rather than the intended target, it had landed squarely nearby, in the obvious neighborhood of my goal. Uncannily close, and yet, not the mark. At all.

Humph. I wondered inwardly. *What was that about?*

There had been so much energy and excitement and vision. What I was aiming for had seemed so crystal clear, I felt certain it would be an absolute bull's-eye. I could *feel* it.

As I pondered this, moving to retrieve my metaphorical arrow, just beyond the target, I took stock of my surround-ings. It was a lovely place. Flowers bloomed on all manner of foliage I'd never encountered before. And yet … something seemed familiar. What was it? There was a niggling in my consciousness.

I recalled a time I'd wholeheartedly pursued a goal. One that seemed completely far-fetched. So crazy that every time I'd written about it in my journal I could only seem to call it "absolutely ridiculous" and yet, I had pursued it. I'd launched multiple arrows towards that target. Each one landed just past it. But I was compelled by something I couldn't see, something deeper, something I didn't try to name, but followed with a childlike joy that accompanies a sense that a wonderful discovery is just around the corner. As the last arrow thumped into the ground and not the target, I completely surrendered my intended outcome.

It just wasn't meant to be. I told myself, by way of explanation and consolation. Yet, there was the energy that had gone into those arrows. Somehow I couldn't believe that all that powerful, exuberant energy had propelled my arrows to nothing.

Life went on, and a mere two months later, there was a major shift in the area of my life where the target had stood. It seemed, those arrows, loosed with love and grounded somewhere beyond the target, had caused ripples on impact. Those ripples moved out and made major changes in my life, far beyond what I could have imagined, and are still affecting my life today in positive ways.

Sometimes, I wonder now, if most times, it's good to miss the mark.

About Rest

sometimes the hardest thing
is stopping to look around
after running fast

L ATELY I'VE BEEN STRUGGLING with a secret.
I've been feeling uninspired and listless. The usual things that bring me an abundance of joy just don't hold any interest for me. I find this alarming.

I confided this to a friend a few days ago. She called to find out how my recent unemployment was going. I confessed to the above feelings of general ennui in my life and how I thought I should be excited to have all this time on my hands to DO the things I previously rarely had time or energy to tackle.

"The one thing I can garner excitement about," my confession continued, "is yoga."

"That's good," my friend encouraged neutrally.

"But," I hesitated, trying to get words around what I was feeling, "shouldn't I want to DO all those things I say I love to do? I'm a writer. Shouldn't I take this time to write? Instead, all I want to do is read."

"You're a writer. Reading is good," she validated.

"Or sculpting," I continued. "I have zero desire to sculpt. I just …" I petered out helplessly.

My friend paused before replying, "Sometimes, it's just about rest." She went on to remind me how stressful the last few years have been for me. And although things are good in my life in general, maybe this time of unemployment was about resting.

Now, I'd like to say here, in support of my loving husband, he has said the same thing to me during the first three weeks of unemployment. But this time I *heard* it. And what allowed me to hear it was framing it in this struggle I've had with NOT doing things I thought I wanted to be doing.

As I wrote about the experience with my friend, I remembered the above haiku that I'd written during a time when I was experiencing immense difficulty with my health. It IS difficult to slow down, no matter what speed one has been going, running or otherwise.

··· •···

I LET THIS ESSAY SIT for a couple of months. I'm glad I did, because sometimes perspective takes time. It is a gorgeous fall day today. The sun is shining, the sky is clear blue, it's in the sixties with a soft breeze, and the trees are still doing that fantastical thing they do this time of year. It is perfect—an easy day to have perspective.

Rest, I did. And sure enough, eventually, the desire to embrace my goals has returned. Each day I sit down to write for fifteen minutes. Some might say that's not much, perhaps not even enough. And it's true. It's not a lot. It's not the thousand words a day my friend is writing on her novel. But it's what I can do. Each day that I can say I've met that fifteen-minute goal is a great day in my mind.

One thing I've learned over the last six years is that little things DO add up. Who knew, when I started writing haiku in 2007, I would inspire and encourage myself to keep up the discipline for this many years? Who knew a simple three lines a week would become over three-hundred published poems? I'm a firm believer in the small and seemingly mundane. I used to think that if I didn't sit for hours pouring out words, it wasn't worth my time. Now I think that by focusing my efforts for a scant fifteen minutes, I'm writing stronger. (Well, I'm certainly writing stronger than if I'd not tried at all!)

I'm glad I listened to my friend (and my husband) and rested when I didn't feel inspired to move on my creative goals. Wherever you are today, I hope you're able to rest if you've been running fast, whatever that looks like for you.

NATURE

Sidewalk Flowers

the sidewalk flower
genuine celebrity
often overlooked

W HAT LOOKS RANDOM and filled with chance, is per-
haps less so than one might think. Take the sidewalk
flower: a seed, all the same potential as any other seed,
lands in a spot deemed by most as highly inauspicious and
inhospitable ... the sidewalk crack.

But then, despite cramped quarters, few nutrients and
armed with nothing but its own enthusiasm for the oppor-
tunity to bloom in this special place, the little seed bursts
from its casing. Wriggling to the surface, a leaf unfurls, a
banner of green vitality and hope; part of the battle is won.
Powered by the momentum of one leaf, two, three, four more
and it's dancing in the wind, reveling in the sunlight, both
the direct and that bouncing off the mica in the cement of
the surrounding concrete.

Many days pass. It focuses its ebullience, the heady impor-
tance of its mission, into the deep rich color of petals to

come … the central ability to reproduce and cross pollinate on the wind or bee's legs, meeting with other flower pollen, like great minds at a Salon-style gathering. Ideas masterful and minor, bumble in their own synergy and exquisite complexity.

Finally, in its glorious completeness, the flower opens shop, right there on the sidewalk, ready to do the business of making someone's day. How many days does it have to carry out this mission? The brevity of its time frame is punctuated by the little plant's desire to garner someone's attention. Daily, it waves its cheery petals in harmony with the breeze. Days and people pass. The sun rises and sets in its own celestial dance with the moon and earth, completing its own duties, part of an unfathomably enormous cog in a mind-blowingly vast system of the universe.

Our little flower friend fades and closes shop for the last time. Its mission fulfilled, if only in retrospect.

Yearning

painterly drop cloths
vermilion and ocher hues
encircle the trees

I DON'T KNOW WHY I try to take pictures. No. I know why I try to take pictures, but I don't know why I continue to do so when the results will never capture what I see. No. That's not true either. The photos capture what I see, but not what I *feel*.

How to capture the color of yearning? How to capture the desire of Soul to touch the face of God?

And yet, that's what I try to do every fall.

Sunlight through fall leaves, golden, amber, ocher, orange, vermillion and the myriad colors between. That is the visual experience that captures something I struggle to put into words the rest of the year. And it's not just the autumn leaves themselves. It's the act of sunlight shining through them that captures the stained-glass cathedral of spiritual yearning in my heart.

When I stop to admire the tree's leaves, I want to become

the experience—that beauty and color and light. A faint tint of disappointment is present as well, for the moment is so ephemeral and fleeting. And it is yearning, for I am never fully absorbed into that gorgeous light. I am looking at it in longing. I am reaching out, trying to *be* it and yet acutely feeling the separateness as well. For the act of yearning is, itself, incomplete. Always stretching its hand out, like Michelangelo's Adam, extending his finger towards God—the space between cradles yearning—both Adam's and God's, perhaps.

Yes. Sunlight through fall leaves is the color of yearning.

Maple Syrup

galvanized buckets
slung like six-shooter holsters
on sugar maples

THE WEEK BEFORE LAST, I looked out the front window
of our house to see a man standing in our driveway.
He carried something in his hands that I couldn't quite
identify. Since we live on the premises of a historic prop-
erty, we are used to strangers standing in our driveway. It
was sub-freezing weather and I was up to my elbows and
eyebrows in a basement reorganization project, so I went
back to it. A short while later I came up from the basement
to ask my husband a question and he mentioned the guy in
front of our house.

"Some guys are hanging maple syrup buckets on the
trees out front."

"They are?! I wondered what that guy was doing out front.
I almost asked him, but it's so cold. Do you think they'd
mind if I went to ask them about it?" A strange giddiness
began to overtake me.

I was already struggling with my snow boots when my husband casually replied. "Sure. I already talked to them. They probably wouldn't mind."

I had my coat on and was donning a hat and mittens. I was out the door before he was. I still had the width of the drive and some length of it to traverse when the question burst from me: "Hi! I'm from Arizona. This is only my second winter in New England. Do you mind if I ask you some questions? I'm really interested in what you're doing!" I felt like I was about seven years old again, struck with a mad curiosity about this seemingly quaint ritual taking place in my own yard.

Both men turned to look as my husband joined me. It was the younger one who spoke. "Sure, no problem. We're tapping the maple trees." The guy began in an easy-mannered tone, explaining, "These are sugar maples. They're the best ones to tap because they yield about a three percent return as opposed to black or red maples that only have a two percent return." He was so confident, yet casual. He continued, "It'll take about forty gallons of sap to make a gallon of syrup."

I felt like I might as well have been talking to an astronaut, my front yard transformed to the surface of the moon or Mars. Awestruck, I asked, "How can you tell this is a sugar maple?"

"By the bark. See how it's lifting here and the way the branches are shaped and taper?" He pointed out a place on the trunk nearest him where the bark curled up and looked up at the naked arms of the tree reaching into the gray sky.

I followed his gaze, trying to see what he was seeing, though I didn't feel I had much success discerning the difference between the branches of the sugar maple and the tree next to it.

"How long will you leave the buckets up?" I asked.

"Well, this is an odd year because it's been so cold," he began. "Normally we would have tapped the trees on the twentieth of February. But we haven't been above freezing, so we couldn't." Then his voice carried hope, "This weekend, we are supposed to get into the forties, which is when the sap will start flowing."

He smiled broadly and continued, "It has to get into the forties during the day and freeze at night in order for the sap to flow. Once it stops freezing at night, we won't be able to collect sap anymore because it will have stopped flowing. The freeze/thaw cycle needs to be present for the sap to flow. Typically, the sap stops flowing about the end of March. But this is an odd year, so who knows."

I watched as he tapped a spile, a metal tube with a spout-shaped end, into the tree trunk where he'd just drilled a hole. His friend followed up by hanging a galvanized metal bucket with a cover onto the spile.

"How do you decide how many buckets to hang on each tree?" I asked, looking at the various number of sap holsters on the nearby trees.

"A tree has to be at least twelve inches in diameter to be tapped. At about eighteen inches you can put two buckets on. And some really big, old trees that I can't get my arms around can have up to four buckets." He was very patient with his answers.

"How do you know where to tap?"

"You can see the big veins if you look at the shape of the tree." He pointed this out on the tree he was tapping.

"Oh yeah…"

"We like tapping on the south side of the tree too, because that means more sun on it and a longer flow time during the day," he offered up before they moved to the next tree. "We'll come by at the end of the day to collect the sap."

Despite the fact they'd kept working as I peppered them with questions, I felt I'd held them up long enough. "Thanks for taking the time to tell us all about this! It's so neat to see it happening in our front yard." I grinned like a fool and headed back to the warmth of the house.

The weather hasn't gotten warm enough on most days since the inaugural tapping for the sap to flow every day. On one forty-plus day, we returned from a walk in the late afternoon, and, like a child checking for presents on Christmas morning, I ran to inspect the bucket nearest us, lifting its lid. Sure enough, it held a small amount of clear liquid. Having grown up around pine trees, I expect sap to be sticky, slow moving and colored; I was surprised by its clarity and fluidity.

We stood in the stillness and listened. There was a quiet, persistent tap … tap … tap coming from the tree next to us. I was awed by this singular sound of waking trees and spring's approach.

Idyllic

tiny white flutters
sun-warmed impossible green
flashing scarlet wings

I THINK PERHAPS next year I shall embrace my old nemesis winter with a heartfelt hug. Without its chilly, white contrast, the vibrancy of spring might not make the impression upon me it has.

As a lover of autumn, I used to sort of sneer at people who thought spring the best season. I imagined them to be the type of folk who are perennially cheery, annoyingly chipper and dare I say it, unfailingly hopeful.

Maybe as a lover of autumn I tend to cling too long to the "what was" in anticipation and slight dread of the "what is coming."

This year, I have been experiencing spring in a whole new way—one that I suspect most others, over the time we've existed as human's have—the way that inspires stories of rebirth, renewal, and poetry.

These days, as my husband and I walk our favorite path,

down Main Street, turning right on Prospect Street, following it until we veer left on River Road and come to our Favorite Field; we will pause and breathe in the idyllic scene before us. Renewed. Rejuvenated. Even, dare I say it, hopeful.

A Name

emerging across
the ocean's dark camouflage
engulfed by a wing

THEIR APPEARANCE was fantastical.
As if the ocean itself departed its moody and watery nature winged by desire. The white and gray of their feathers disguised as the play of light on water—until the moment they revealed themselves, flying a few feet from where we stood, riveted, on the sand. Hundreds of piping plovers traveled past us on their way to the dune grass flanking the beach. So well camouflaged, we simply couldn't see them as individuals until they were nearly upon us.

··· • ···

I LOVE THE NAMES GIVEN TO GROUPS of animals. I recently learned that while a group of fish is a school, a school of goldfish is called a troubling! (And a baby fish is a fry.) I learned this marvelous tidbit from a children's book I thumbed through at work the other day. (*How Things Work in the House* by Lisa Campbell Ernst)

In looking up names for creatures with which I feel an affinity, I sought out the name for a group of seahorses. Some said it was herd—to which I say, "Yawn."

Others said it should be school.

Puhleaze, I'm asleep already. (Guess they'd never heard of the specialized troubling for goldfish.) And so I put forth my own name for a gathering of seahorses: a whimsy.

And now to "a wing," used in this week's haiku. A wing is a group of piping plovers in flight. Not in-flight, they are a congregation.

Here are a few of my favorite group nouns:

Hippopotamuses travel in a bloat.

Porcupines a prickle.

Cockroaches an intrusion, (ya think?)

Jellyfish a smack.

Giraffes? A tower, (of course!)

What's in a name? Turns out it's often a giggle (not to be confused with a gaggle), and some great imagery.

Introducing Lotta

barefooted dancing
Lotta rain kissed the desert
longing for flowers

WHILE WINTER BRINGS BLIZZARDS, whiteouts, ice storms and all manner of snowy accumulations to many parts of the world, rain is the winter offering laid at the feet of the Sonoran Desert in the Southwestern U.S. Like its frozen counterpart, winter rain in the arid west brings spring flowers.

Blossoming from a Siri boo-boo during this rainy season, my friend introduced me to "Lotta." (Thank you Amy!) Imagination grabbed Lotta's hand and danced off with her directly.

··· •···

SPINDLY BUCKHORN CHOLLA dropped five branches. A nearby prickly pear dropped a pad joined by a teddybear cactus branch of long, golden spines catching sunlight. Cottontail bunny nibbled appreciatively nearby, it's fuzzy pelt snagging on spines. By morning the dew had felted its shed fur to the spindly buckhorn. An unlikely collection of desert detritus when viewed dead on, the mind discards the pile as a pointless jumble, a thing to be overlooked and forgotten. In the periphery we see …

A slip of a girl, Lotta, is born of the desert for the love of flowers—a sprite of the spring. With buckhorn cholla limbs, she stands. Her footsteps are a feathery touch upon the rain-starved dirt. Her face is the picture of bliss with a supremely serene smile. Her hair hangs in two long braids. She dances, barefoot among the cacti, bending, jumping, light feet kissing the dusty earth that delights in the tickling touch of her toes.

She dances for what might be. As her arms extend, she imagines flowers here and there, everywhere her fingers pointing the many ways. She giggles a bit, then laughs more heartily with a depth belying the belly of her small frame. It builds and booms, echoing off the far-off surrounding mountains.

In her wake, a fresh scent rests on the land. It is the smell of gratitude and things to come.

Note: Buckhorn cholla, prickly pear and teddybear are just a few of the three-hundred species of cacti found in the diverse Sonoran Desert.

PURE QUIRK

Slippery Fish

peripheral glimpse
rainbow-slick unconscious flash
slippery fish dreams

THIS MORNING, my dreams are slippery fish. Standing knee deep in the water of my dream consciousness, feet planted in a pebbly riverbed, toes digging into the more sandy spots, still firmly planted in sleep. Yet my head is out here, firing on sips of coffee, my pen poised to dart in after those rainbow-flashing fish.

I see them in my periphery. Undulating slick rainbows, biding their time in the current. But whether I am too slow to catch them, or the water distorts their location, when my pen touches paper, the fish dart away.

I refocus my attention elsewhere, the rainbow slippery flashes again in my periphery, perhaps if I don't look at them straight on, I will land one out here on paper—my pen the fishing spear.

This morning, however, there is no dream catch to pen in my journal, only the phrase, "slippery fish dreams." Perhaps tomorrow I will plate a fine dream image on the perfectly white page of my journal, capturing its likeness brought to me by the me that is deeper than Now, truer than True. The self that knows I Know, the self that IS ... and I will feed my insatiable curiosity to know more about the vast internal landscape of my beingness.

Absolute Detachment

stretching to see more
with absolute detachment
joyfully engaged

THERE IT WAS: A large prickly pear cactus whose gorgeous blooms glowed in the morning sunlight. I longed to see the floral springtime creations, but the crown of flowers was well over my head. All I could see was the light shining through the petals.

I grabbed my phone and with my sneaker-clad feet balanced on *en point*, arms stretched high, I blindly snapped a photo. In that moment, I managed to summon the recipe for Absolute Detachment. I freely share it here:

> 1 part Buoyant hopefulness (use Fully Open Heart brand)
>
> 1 part Utter "this probably won't work" (Don't confuse this with Total Pessimism, it's similar, but not the same. As you might guess, Total Pessimism is more bitter.)
>
> 1 dash I-Gotta-Try!

The sun was too bright to see the photo on my phone. I always wait until I'm sipping coffee at the Desert Botanical Gardens' wonderful restaurant before I examine the day's photographic catch. In the shade of a canvas umbrella, with the fountain burbling next to me, I flip through my photos. This morning, the only one I find truly captivating is the over-the-head shot of the prickly pear flowers.

There is a balance to the composition that I would doubtfully have achieved if I'd tried. I love the surprise visit of the bee and other flying insect enjoying the pollen, as well as the four stages of the flower. Frayed petals move backward through time to newly opened, not-yet-opened and working-into-the-bud. I love the strong diagonal of the cactus pads reaching from top to bottom. And I am especially fond of the shadows in the dirt background formed by the nearby ocotillo-branch ramada.

Being detached conjures images of cool aloofness, a separateness that indicates a strong Us-and-Them mentality where the world is viewed from afar. But this detachment was nothing like that. The I-ness of me disappeared and I joyfully engaged fully with my surroundings. Most importantly, I had no attachment to the outcome. In the moment I snapped that image, without trying, I mastered the above recipe for Absolute Detachment.

Now, where else can that be applied in life?

MARBLE/marble

"you're gonna be great!"
thinking of Chet makes me smile
good stone memories

I RECENTLY CORRESPONDED with my sculpting mentor. He's going to MARBLE/marble this week and if I were still in Colorado, I'd be going with him. It's difficult for me to believe six years have passed since I was introduced to that part of myself I now know as a sculptor. I miss it. I'd be lying if I said I didn't. Indeed, discovering myself as a sculptor was tantamount to discovering I'd had a third arm all along. No one could have been more astonished than I.

At the moment, I have no way or place to sculpt. In lieu of that, I mark the spot in my heart with this haiku and the essay I wrote about my introduction to stone sculpting—a week at MARBLE/marble sculpting symposium in the heart of the Colorado Rockies.

··· • ···

THE PROBLEM WITH TRYING to write about MARBLE/marble is that it's like trying to look into the sun. All I can really do is squint at it, or look askance, then blink and try to make sense of what I see around me. Because after looking at the sun, everything looks different.

For the week I'm there I dream of sculpture. I dream of sculpting. These are not my everyday dreams. These are fevered dreams. I am working on sculpture all night long so that there is no sleep, only the feeling and vision of sculpting. The pillow is marble and I'm shaping, shaping, shaping it. These nighttime images stay with me for a full week when I return from the artistic retreat.

Re-entry is difficult. I am homesick for Marble, for tents, for cold nights and warm beds, for marbleslab breakfast on a cliff overlooking the swirling Crystal River with the upside down tree that defies gravity and sense by growing in its own mad beautiful way in a place I've come to equate with love and laughter and growth and smiles and eyes whose color change and I cannot look away. It is this simple; I fell in love daily.

My first impression of MARBLE/marble is of Josh's huge brown eyes like a Byzantine painting and arms covered with white marble dust. His passion for stone emanated forth from his beingness. He carves giant quarry blocks into bite-sized sculptor bits. I found out later he is Madeline's son. His wife Gia and their son Anders and daughter Savannah were there as well. Three generations sculpting in the woods of the Crystal River Valley. There are people, tents, marble blocks and energy everywhere. It's like no place I've ever been and not what I imagined. I am excited. Overwhelmed. Overjoyed. This is a place where magic happens.

Madeline pilots the program and the bobcat forklift. Her smile flashes light and happiness from the shadows of the cockpit. She is real. Vibrant. Alive and loving. She deftly wields tons of stone to and fro all over the camp. People are bustling around creating open-air studios, seeking out their stones and greeting one another. For many this is a reunion. For Rebekah, MARBLE/marble is family. She is fifteen, and all black and kohl, all talk and brains. She is a mile-a-minute—nonstop. Feisty and funny, I immediately take a shine to her and we are fast friends. She's been coming here her whole life—practically born here. Her parents, Rex and Vicki are instructors and were part of the first MARBLE/marble experience eighteen years ago.

Fifteen years ago Bob, my mentor, came to this symposium not much farther along in his sculpting career than I am. He's been coming back every year. Madeline saves his spot by the river and this year there is a spot saved for me there as well. I am honored. Later that day, I find out from Mike, a man whose face has launched a thousand Westerns, that Bob is known to many as "The Gentleman Carver." I laugh when I hear this as it suits him perfectly. Always impeccable in clean chinos, long-sleeved button-down shirts, suspenders and a white straw hat, Bob saunters down to his studio by nine thirty every morning. He is quiet and affable and I can't for the life of me figure out how he stays so clean.

The rest of us will be covered, head to toe, in marble dust and yet Bob manages to stay pristine and unruffled. He is a lovely man who produces lovely sculpture.

By the end of the first day sculpting I pen these words in my journal:

> MY GOD! WHAT A PLACE!
>
> People here are so encouraging. The kindness is sweet and touching.
>
> I am in LOVE, LOVE, LOVE!
>
> I smile at everyone.

At the end of the second day carving I'm looking for excuses to get away from my so-called sculpture and having serious doubts that the bedding plane is going the correct way. I'm feeling tired mentally and physically, and I'm wondering just what the hell I've gotten myself into here. My mind roils with phrases like: *I'm an imposter! I don't know anything about sculpting! I'm not an artist!*

It's about this time that Chet comes over to introduce himself. Fantastic good fun, he is a retired orthopedic surgeon from Las Vegas. The sculpture he's working on is an abstract female figure that I just adore. It's cubistic in form yet still accessible and inviting. Later in the week a friend points out that Chet's hair goes left his body leans right, and wouldn't he make a great sculpture? But on day two, I am not yet to the point of seeing everything as a sculpture, so when Chet offers to help me see my piece in the hunk of stone before me, I am grateful for his guidance. I'm so new to this process I don't even know what questions to ask. When he leaves I have a much better idea how to block out my piece.

As it turns out, it is impossible to easily and quickly block one's piece without the use of serious power tools. For this I turn to one of the instructors. Cathi is gorgeous, with healthy, sun-drenched, patinaed skin and sparkling eyes. She is powerful with a nine-inch side grinder. Get outta her way! It is wielded like an extension of her arms. She is sleek and confident and immensely talented. She makes some of the first cuts on my piece, smacking them out with a hammer. Her poise with the power tools must be infectious because by the end of the day I pick up the nine-inch side grinder without a guard on it and lop away big pieces of marble.

Day four rolls around and I'm tired of everyone's good intentions. I'm so overwhelmed with advice that I become paralyzed. I find myself wandering over to the cul-de-sac where Ellen's working on her "Twisty Bunny" piece. Ellen was a Disney animator for twenty years. She quit last fall and moved to Loveland, Colorado, to pursue a career in sculpting. This is her third stone sculpture. Her maquette is flawless. She is paralyzed in her own way so we chat for a bit about marble intimidation and the fear of cutting off something important. Next to Ellen is Western Mike, who seems to have no paralysis happening at all, and across from her is Barry. I've found my man. Barry has sharp blue eyes and wit to match. He is brilliantly funny and hands down the best motivational speaker at Marble this year.

The blue of his eyes is enhanced by the marble dust on

his forehead when he removes his goggles and dust mask to speak. I hope to always hear his voice when I get to the point of giving up, "Oh yeah! You gotta just go for it! Don't worry about what it looks like. Just go do your thing. Become the tip of the chisel." He is in love with the stone and the process, and I catch it.

It is with those words that I approach my stone. Again. Struggling. I look at it this way and that. Chet comes over again, animated, agitated, and points out the obvious. DING! The light goes on. I can see it. I can see what he's talking about. Those big huge hunks HAVE to come off in order for the form to emerge.

"Do that and you'll *really* feel like you've done something today, Girl. Yeah. You're gonna be great! Now just do that! Move that stone!" I didn't exactly become one with the tip of the chisel, but I definitely became one with the nine-inch grinder, and when the dust had settled, I had a much more recognizable seahorse before me.

The last few days I worked on my piece and took time to walk around and chat with the people I've come to call my Marble family. Our litmus question for how the day was going became, "Are you coming back next year?" By the last day my answer was a firm, "Heck yeah!" When I was packing up to leave, people came by to say how amazed they were at the work I got done, and on my first try, and wasn't the belly looking round, and they could really see the head and I felt happy. And content.

I went to MARBLE/marble to learn to sculpt and I fell

in love. Daily. With the people, the place, the process, and always the stone. That beautiful mesmerizing, glowing, glittering marble from the heart of the Rockies. It is bewitching. The dance of the stone is divine.

Reality

subtle shift sideways
alternate reality
made-up memories

I GOT IN PAUL'S CAR. He's my "other brother"—the one my parent's call their foster son. He is my brother's friend, but spent a lot of time with our family when I was in high school, college and my twenties.

Paul had a late '70s Chevette and was letting me borrow it. I think I was in my freshman year of college, home for the holidays and without wheels. I adjusted the seat and mirrors, then reached for the gearshift, a gorgeous hand-carved piece of cherry wood. It was carved in a rounded T-shape that meant the cross bar of the T fit perfectly in the palm of the hand, and the perpendicular trunk of the letter was attached to the gear lever. *Man, that's really cool,* I thought. It totally fit my brother Paul, and it made me idolize him even more and wonder what friend had made it for him.

A couple of years went by. Paul and I were going to see a movie or do something else when we were both home, and I got in the passenger side of his Chevette. It still smelled the same—an earthy blend of garlic (my brothers often traveled together, camping out of Paul's car, so that it usually smelled of food), coffee, sage, herb and male mystique. I smiled. It was always good to get to spend time with Paul. I looked down at his gearshift and was horrified to find a hideous, common, stock, amorphous, black plastic blob of a knob.

"What happened to that really cool, hand-carved gear-shift knob that looked like it was cherry wood?" I gasped.

Paul looked at me with a furrowed brow. "What gearshift? I've never had anything but this."

"No. C'mon. I'm serious. That thing was so cool. I was going to ask you who made it."

Paul, humoring me, "What did it look like?"

"You know, it was sort of curvy T-shape and fit your hand really well, like they made it for you." I was sure he was messing with me.

"Huh. That sounds really cool. But I never had anything like that." He shrugged and laughed. "Are you sure you're not thinking of someone else's car?" He started the Chevette and we moved away from the curb in front of my parents' house.

"No! I noticed and admired it when I borrowed your car that time—at Christmas. Remember?" I was feeling kinda annoyed at this point.

"Yeah ..." he paused to look at me, "but I never had anything like that."

"Wow. That's really weird." And I let it drop. But it made me feel funny, like I remembered a totally different reality from everyone else. And maybe I did. I had a year in there where I experimented with drugs …

A few weekends ago I was reminded of this experience when I rendezvoused with my family for Paul's wedding to Rowshan. My sister mentioned in passing that the blog I'd written about her being featured in the local paper—with a photo showing her drying her waist-length hair over the air conditioner—was a great fabrication.

"What do you mean? You were in the paper that time, remember?" I defended.

"Ah, no Baby Doll," she said, using her nickname for me, "I wasn't." She laughed.

Horrified, "You weren't?! Are you sure? I remember the black and white image …"

"Well, I dried my hair like that, sure. But I was never in the paper."

"Really?" I crinkled the right side of my face—the only side I can wink with. "Really? I don't know. It was a piece about saving energy. It was the seventies!" Slightly hysterical for my obviously slipping sanity, I added "I'm going to go ask Jimmy!"

Laughing, she said, "Okay. I really don't think I was in the paper though."

GAH! I've lied online, in my blog! Jimmy will clear this up. He'll totally back me.

I rushed out to the living room of the bed and breakfast where I found our brother Jimmy sitting with his laptop trying to buy a motorcycle helmet.

"Hey, do you remember that time when Beth was in the paper, blow drying her hair over the air conditioner. You know, it was in *The Progress* ..." I filled in more details of the glossy black-and-white image.

Jimmy looked up, squinted across the distance of his memory. "Yeah..." he paused, and I took heart. "Well, I remember her blow drying her hair that way, because, you know, we all did. You'd go outside," he made a great sound like industrial hair dryer meets blast oven, "and your hair would be dry." He laughed. "But ... I don't remember it being in the paper." He noticed my face, "I mean, maybe. You should ask Mom and Dad. It sounds kinda familiar. They'd know for sure, though." He smiled that blue-eyed smile.

"Yeah. I guess. Man. That is so *weird*." And that's when the memory of the gearshift in my other brother's car came back to me. Along with another memory, from much earlier in my life, about feeding sardines to seals at a zoo with my family—the vendor's cart, its red and white striped awning, the paper tray the sardines were sold in, the seal habitat—and my mother assuring me we'd never done anything of the sort.

So I took a minute to fill my brother in on my theory of the alternate reality, which, by my experience is not a theory but a, well, reality. He didn't totally buy it. But he didn't pooh-pooh it either.

Then I shared that my husband was experiencing this as well.

We have two cats. I'll call them Pumpkin and Peanut. Peanut has always had sweet little tufts that stick out just behind her ears. Pumpkin does not. He has a ruff, but not any tufts.

Until about a month ago.

"Ohmygod! Peanut's tufts are gone!" I exclaimed to my husband, a very sane, rational, logical man.

"No ..." He came over to check them out. "Ohmygod! You're right! Where did they go? Did she shed them?" After all, it was summer.

"Maybe, but I don't remember her ever losing them before. How does that happen?" We both loved her tufts. I'd even written a haiku about them.

> purring Peanut sports
> ridiculous long whiskers
> and soft, tufty ears

A few minutes later, my husband exclaimed, "Look at Pumpkin! He's got tufts! And they're gray!" Pumpkin is black. Peanut is grey. How did one cat lose tufts and the other gain them?

"See? Alternate realities." I concluded to my brother Jimmy, "And now my husband is experiencing it too." I raised my eyebrows conspiratorially.

He laughed. "Yeah, that's pretty wild." He laughed some more. "Well, you always have had a great memory for dreams and the other worlds."

I'll add at this juncture that there are no drugs involved in my life—not for well over twenty years. I'm not convinced, as some people have indicated, that it's just my mind making things up. I really do believe we are only a hair's breadth away from worlds other than our own.

Oh. And my parents agreed with my siblings. My sister was never featured in *The Scottsdale Progress* blow-drying her hair over the air conditioning compressor unit. At least not in the *current* reality.

The Exuberance

the exuberance
of a well-written haiku
this is not that week

WHAT HAPPENED that Thursday?
I wrote exactly what I was processing.

I had another haiku started. One that was spiritual and uplifting and deep. One that I was trying hard to feel and wanted to feel, but I just couldn't quite make the last few steps to the summit and gain clarity. The first two lines I really liked, they got me most of the way up the mountain. But the third line, no matter what I wrote, it felt trite and bogus.

I don't know if that haiku will ever see the light of day outside my journal, and that's okay. What I'm most interested in is what happened in the three lines that *did* get sent.

the exuberance

I gotta say, I'm not sure where this came from. The word exuberance popped into my mind while I was casting about the week for fodder since line three of the other haiku wasn't working. The final line had all the character and truth of a mal-formed plastic toy whose only clear message was the stamp reading, "Made in China."

Exuberance! Shouted its way into my mind and I jotted it down thinking, *this could be workable*, as I counted syllables.

The next two lines came in nearly simultaneously as I thought about how this week had been void of writing—I'd been too busy with a sizeable problem that had been sitting on my plate for far too long—a half-eaten, indigestible elephant I'd been trying to chomp one bite at a time.

Once again, my inner critic barked discouraging words in the background. I wanted so badly to rally. To ignore the problematic plate I'd been choking on, to pen something worthwhile. And so, the last two lines came out feeling like a simple equation. Line one plus line two equals, simply, line three.

As with plenty of the haiku that get flung across cyberspace to kind readers, this one drew a number of replies. Humblingly, my truth, born in the moment of my attempt to capture it in words, touched others. One reply in particular set me to pondering.

Maybe we *are* at our strongest when we are our most vulnerable. Maybe in the moment of attempting to speak, write, paint, sculpt, create our truth, we open ourselves to something larger and greater than ourselves, and *that* is what people respond to. Maybe ... it's not the words, the book, the painting, the sculpture, the whatever, but the *intent* behind it that matters most.

ALL THE LOVE AROUND US

Lifeboat

audio lifeboat
sailed across many miles
on currents of love

IN THE FALL OF 2010, I found myself in one of the darkest wells I'd inhabited yet. Try as I might, I was having no amount of success pulling myself out of the depression. And, I was headed into the worst time of the year for me—winter. The short days, long nights, and often cloud-laden days, wreak havoc on my brain chemistry.

As I faced winter 2010–2011, I was worried about myself, and my ability to hold back the darkness. I was more concerned than I'd been in a decade.

As a gift for my birthday at the end of September, a dear friend of mine had taken the time to compile a wonderful CD with an eclectic selection of music. As I listened to it that first morning, on my way to a job that for reasons best explained in a different venue, felt like a prison to me, I was transported away from my life. I thought of her and our wonderful friendship. I thought about things other than myself, and the weights in my life that pulled me downward. I was buoyed in a way I'd been unable to attain for myself.

When I arrived at work, in a moment completely uncharacteristic to me, I reached out. I composed an email to a few close friends who knew me well enough that I could express my vulnerability and fear. I also knew these friends had vast libraries of music that I didn't. This was an important part of the rescue plan. All my music was old and worn to me. It was frayed around the edges and brought me no solace. Most of it would, in fact, transport me to another time and place in my life. That wasn't helpful to me.

I needed to be reminded of dear friends and love. I was convinced that as I listened to new music from old friends, I would wear new, happier thought patterns, like grooves in a record, into my brain and beingness. Some, if not all of these friends, had struggled themselves with depression at some point or another. I knew they would understand my plea for help.

Reaching out so boldly scared me a little, but I sent the email.

The first to arrive was a package that to this day brings tears of gratitude to my eyes. It was from Lee whom I knew, from back in the days when we had cassette players in our cars, liked to make mixed tapes. Today, she is a busy, working mom—active in all kinds of endeavors. It was, and remains, a miracle to me that she put this package together at all, let alone as swiftly as she did.

To get to the CD, I had to open an envelope on which

she had written, "Lalee is…" surrounded by twenty-one adjectives and phrases that made me cry so much when I first saw them, it took me twenty minutes to get myself together enough to open the envelope. Inside, I discovered not one, but six CDs. Each had an image of us, taken from her personal scrapbook, on the sleeve. I cried even more when I looked at each one.

The next morning on my way to work, I began my journey through the six CDs. Beginning with Maroon 5's version of Willy Wonka's "Pure Imagination" and ending with U2's "Some Days Are Better Than Others," the first CD is like a surreptitious note passed during a dreary middle-school social studies class. It's a funny, sweet, brilliant, lifesaver. Discs two through six run the gamut from putting a boogie in my butt, to deeply spiritual and healing—making me want to invest in myself in every way.

Over the next month, discs came in from NYC, Washington DC, and Jackson, Wyoming. Those audio lifeboats got me through the next few months to spring and another opportunity to find balance yet again.

Undying gratitude to you who sent CDs—I love you all more than words can say. And now you can say, you saved someone's life.

Falling in Love

baby lima beans
A Wrinkle in Time *and more*
gifts from my sister

I'M BOR-ED," my ten-year-old self whines to my older sister as she finishes brushing her gorgeous, waist-length, honey-colored hair.

"Go read a book," she advises sagely, looking in my direction via the mirror.

I crinkle my face and frown. "A bo-ok? (the whining still present) "I don't have any books to read."

With infinite patience she guides me into her room and pulls a hardback book off the shelf. "Here, read this. It's a really good book, you're going to love it!" She smiles encouragingly.

I look at the blue cover. Concentric green and black circles surround the white silhouettes of three figures in various places on the cover. "A Wrinkle in Time?" I ask, utterly unconvinced. "Just *try* it. You might *like* it." She says kindly.

I slouched back to my room, highly doubtful something

with the word *wrinkle* in the title had the power to save me from the oppressive doom of boredom. Flopping down on my bed, I turned pages to reach the first page whose chapter was titled, "Mrs. Whatsit."

It was a dark and stormy night …

Thus began a lifelong love affair with novels, reading, and writing. I had not really gotten into full-length, well-written novels before that afternoon when my sister guided me to one of the best and most loved children's novels of all time. I still go back from time to time and reread Madeleine L'Engle's first book in the trilogy.

Thank you for that marvelous gift, Bethie.

Lima beans. One might think that was a childhood story as well. But no. A couple of years ago I was visiting my family in Arizona. I'd walked over from my folks' house to visit my sister and her husband. It was lunchtime and my sister was just finishing her meal.

"Whadja have?" I inquired, because I was feeling a bit peckish.

"Baby lima beans and …"

"Lima beans? You eat lima beans?" Humph. We hadn't grown up eating lima beans!

"*Baby* lima beans." She replied, "They're good. You can have what's left."

Not since my childhood had I felt such a surge of petulance and reluctance. *Try lima beans! Preposterous! I hate lima beans!* And then I wondered, *Do I really? I don't know that …*

Try them I did. I love them! My husband and I routinely add baby lima beans to our dinner menu.

Thank you, Bethie, for introducing me to a new vegetable and reminding me it's good to stretch one's culinary boundaries.

Of course, I always loved my sister; she's my sister. But I didn't *fall* in love with her until I was thirty-nine.

We planned a road trip together. I had always wanted to drive up the Pacific Coast Highway—it was on my list of Things To Do Before I Leave the Planet. (I'd begun compiling the list years ago in a journal gifted by a friend that featured the character Death from the Sandman graphic novel series by Neil Gaiman.) I'd urged my sister to start a list of her own. When we compared notes, it turned out we had some things in common. And so we met in Los Angeles, rented a car, and spent the next week together driving up the coast in a Pontiac. We'd hoped for a convertible, but our budget only allowed for a sunroof.

> tentative bonding
> sharing laughter and coffee
> miles bring us closer

I learned so much about my sister on that road trip. She doesn't eat much breakfast. She likes to drive fast. She was always game to stop at any beach to help me comb for beach glass. (I treasure my beach glass collection for this reason.) She likes jewelry and shopping. She's the most culinarily adventuresome person I know (I really admire that about her). She is generous and funny and kind. She still loves to read. We shared laughter and tears on that trip. It was the first time, as adults, we'd spent any length of time together without family around. Such a lovely gift.

Steel Steed

automotive taps
timing belt catastrophe
pastures my steel steed

His name was Sognatore. I was deep into my Italo-
phile phase and headed to Italy the following fall after
I got him. So my new-to-me Honda Civic's name became
Sognatore (pronounced: son-ya-tor-ay), Italian for "dreamer"
in the masculine form.

It was September 1999. I was just back to my home state
of Arizona from Washington DC, where I'd been in grad-
uate school for two years. I had sold my previous car (RIP
dear little Spud Car, a chocolate brown 1981 Honda Civic)
before moving to DC two years earlier. As an inhabitant of
the great, wide-open West, I needed a vehicular device. The
silver 1997 DX seemed perfect. It had a ski and bike rack on
the top (a harbinger of my life to come), ten-CD disc changer
in the back (Is that wise in a hatchback?), had low miles and
was the right price.

Two things made me feel the car was meant for me:

The license plate was ADA 234. My first thought was of Ada County, Idaho, where Boise is located. I'd spent many a summer vacation in Boise and the Sawtooth Mountains visiting my mom's family.

"Did you notice the license plate?" I whispered to Mom who, along with Daddy, was on the scouting-cum-buying trip.

"Mm-hmm," she smiled conspiratorially. "Ada County." We nodded knowingly to one another.

The other thing about the car's history was kismet: The girl who was selling it didn't want to, but she was headed back East to go to grad school and didn't need a car where she was going.

It felt like two pieces of a puzzle coming together.

I started the car and backed into the street. It made the same sound my former Civic had made while backing up; like a wind-up toy. Ah ... instant familiarity. I drove it cautiously around the block, noting the fancy stereo whose face twisted out to greet me upon starting and turned back around to hide itself when I turned the car off. Coy little thing.

"Whadya think?" Daddy asked me when I returned.

I smiled, "Pretty nice ..."

And that was that.

Our first road trip was 1,288 unforgettable miles. I was meeting friends from grad school in Fort Davis, Texas, for New Year's Eve 2000. The friend who had organized the trip decided that if Y2K were to go down, she wanted to be in a safe, untouchable place. Fort Davis? My friend had worked at McDonald Observatory and deemed it the only place to be should all electronic devices come to their circuitry demise. (Truth: The stars *are* bright, deep in the heart of Texas!) Fort Davis proved a perfect host and Sognatore and I got to know each other well after those twenty-some-odd hours of driving.

Many of the 176,000 miles we did together were long road trips. From Denver to Scottsdale, Arizona (multiple times), Cheyenne and Jackson, Wyoming, Ojo Caliente, New Mexico, Kearny, Nebraska, down to Puerto Peñasco, Mexico, and up the coast of California to Santa Barbara. Shorter travels took us all over Colorado and northern mountains of Arizona. Never once did he protest.

Denver was not kind to Sognatore however. He seemed to have a target on him, visible only to malicious strangers. The first break in happened January of 2002. I discovered the ten-CD disc changer (with all those CDs!) was missing after a long, hard day of wrestling with a Sawzall at my museum exhibition construction job. Was I mad!

Next was the urban pioneer phase—we were toughing it out in an up-and-coming crack neighborhood. One busted side view mirror, two smashed windows (driver and passenger) and two stereos. It would have been three, but when they demolished the window the last time, the stereo wasn't even in the car. That was the day before I was moving to a newly purchased condo (with a safe garage!) in Boulder. All that abuse in two years.

Our last move to Denver brought a final break-in.

Returning from a morning away, my husband asked, "Where did you park your car?"

Flummoxed, "Where I always park it. Where's my car?" Sognatore was definitely NOT where I had parked him the night before, where he had been when we left the house that morning, next to the house.

Pulling past the house and making a U-turn at the corner where we lived, we saw him parked up the street.

"Did you park there?" My husband queried.

Inwardly I faltered. *Did I? Why would I park up the street, across the way?* Sometimes I'm so slow. I simply could not fathom how Sognatore had made his way to the neighbor's house.

We parked and went to investigate. The sunscreen had been removed from the front dash windshield area and his steering column had been savagely ripped away leaving carnage like a neck wound.

Who steals a car only to leave it fifty yards from whence it came?!

I'll never know. I just figured the perp got in the car for … parts? A dare? Clandestine drug transaction? And decided no power steering, manual transmission and crank windows weren't worth the time. By the time they'd discovered no joy in that ride, they ditched him after having gone around the corner. Sognatore got fixed up (even adding window tint to the last broken window that got replaced but not tinted) and we were on our way once again.

In retrospect, I felt all the break-ins and thefts were about a karmic debt I had to pay in Denver. It seems too much of a coincidence that the times I lived outside Denver, Sognatore was never violated as he was while living there. But I also view everything that happens to me, especially my car, as an extension of my inner spiritual life. All this added to his faithful steed status.

Salvage Saturday arrived. The sky was heavy with clouds that were predicted to bring us four to six more inches of snow. (We'd had a blizzard a few weeks earlier whose two-foot remains were still very evident.) The man from the salvage company called about fifty minutes prior to our agreed time of nine a.m. and we scrambled to get out the door to clear my belongings out of Sognatore.

I posed for a photo, hugging Sognatore to the best of my ability, arms spread to engulf one edge of the windshield and the roof. We emptied the glove box and scoured under the seats for belongings. When that was done, I sat with my arms wrapped around his steering wheel, forehead resting in the center and sobbed like a baby while I told him how much I loved him, appreciated all he'd done for me. For the safe trips, the karma he'd taken for me, and the thirteen years, four months and fifteen days of dedicated service.

When I lifted my head, I saw my tears on the steering wheel and was struck by how tears and tough goodbyes are the sign of a life well loved and lived together. If I'd hated Sognatore, I might have kicked a tire on his way out, shaken my fist and said, "Good riddance!"

I realized too how his passing was so much like our

relationship—no drama. He got me home that last Friday night, we parked in the driveway and he just didn't start the next morning. Sognatore was like that. Reliable. Unassuming. Brave.

Thank you my fine silvery steed. Heart and soul of a horse in a Honda body—I'll miss you my friend.

Heart of an Explorer

helping me explore
the highest mountain around
and deepest canyons

SHORTLY AFTER I HAD MOVED to Colorado, I was hiking in the Rocky Mountains when I saw a young family out for a day hike. One child was young enough to be in a backpack-like child carrier, the other child was probably about five years old and was moving along like a trouper. I was reminded of my own childhood and thought, *What a gift those kids are getting from their parents—what a gift I got from my own parents, especially Daddy …*

Family legend says I got my first pair of hiking boots around age six in preparation for hiking to Havasu Falls in the spring of 1975. In my memory, they were miniature versions of my mom's hiking boots. Clunky, brown leather things with a fair amount of heft to them.

Oh, how I loved them.

A good pair of hiking boots can make one feel invincible. It's true. That's how I felt with my new boots on—and how every subsequent pair I've owned made me feel—or they wouldn't have made it out of the store.

What a silly sight I must have been: skinny little kid legs sprouting from summer shorts or sundresses, with those big ol' "clodhoppers" Dad called them.

Here's what I remember of that ten-mile hike that took us from the rim of one of the tributary canyons of the Grand Canyon on the south side of the Colorado River, to Havasupai Falls:

–Starting out excited. Carrying my own tiny, external frame backpack with all my provisions. (Okay. Likely not food. But water, clothes and sleeping bag.)

–Eating a ton of Mom's homemade beef jerky because I couldn't swallow the salt tablets everyone else was taking in order to stay hydrated. (Man that stuff was gooood!)

–The fantastic falls themselves. An aqua-turquoise blue that brazenly defies all desert convention.

–Complaining. Yep. I was mighty tired with that weighty backpack on. At some point, I think on the trip out of the canyon, my things were dispersed leaving me unencumbered.

Like a bookend to my youth, Dad and his friend, Walt, organized a hike to summit the highest point in the Lower 48 during the summer between my junior and senior year in high school. At 14,505 feet, Mount Whitney is the crowning peak in the Sierra Nevada range, the geological backbone of California. There were nine people in our hiking group, I invited three friends and Daddy had four friends.

We started the morning of our summit at beautiful Guitar

Lake (elevation 11,460 feet), but by the time we reached the crest (elevation 13,600 feet) where we would drop our heavy backpacks and complete the final two miles to reach Whitney, I was already having trouble with the thin air. My pals hiked faster than I was able, so Dad hung back to keep me company. Once we arrived at the peak, I was so hurt to be left behind by my friends, I had worked myself into a fine teenage-tizzy. I found myself gasping for air as I sobbed uncontrollably.

Daddy did his best to calm me. I managed to stop crying and catch my breath. (This was the first time I fully understood the phrase "gasping for air"—there just was so little!) We signed the book at the top and admired the view together.

In retrospect, I'm glad I couldn't keep up with my friends. Dad stayed with me all the way down to our campsite. We made a game of counting each of the ninety-nine switchbacks that descend from Trail Crest, where we had left our packs, to Trail Camp.

Thank you Daddy, for all the hikes and the memories, but most of all for instilling in me a deep love of the wilderness, and teaching me what it takes to get there and back.

A Poet

reassuring words
one poet to another
from Grandpa to me

IN SEPTEMBER, my cousin visited my parents in Arizona. She brought with her four, tome-like photo albums filled with family history. Inside were treasures I spent hours pouring over with Mom when I was back visiting two weeks ago. I saw pictures of my mom as a baby and a young girl.

In the hours I spent studying the images I felt I soul traveled to another time and place. The turn of the last century (nineteenth to twentieth) with my great-grandmother in front of the North Carolina farm where my grandpa grew up, and where my grandma spent her first year of marriage when Grandpa was off driving ambulances in World War I. My aunt's college days during the '30s and her schoolmates. Clippings of my grandpa's poetry from the Huntington, West Virginia, newspaper. Things I'd never seen, people I'd never known or barely met, were there in black and white snapshots. My mother and her brother at Virginia Beach.

Wedding announcements in the Huntington newspaper for my other aunt's wedding. Even my own kindergarten through second-grade school portraits. Family history viewed through my aunt's scrapbooking.

I enjoyed the opportunity to get to know my aunt a little bit, posthumously—she died when I was seven. Among the clippings, I came across two stanzas taken from Grandpa's poetry that spoke to me across the ages.

The first stanza that captured my attention, is the final in a poem called "I Dreamed." I know he wrote it sometime after 1940 and before 1963 when he first published his poems as a book titled *Shadows and Sunshine*. He must have written the poem after age forty-six, as he was born in 1894. He states, in the intro to the book, that the poems are "a mirror that reflects life as I have viewed it from the western side of the hill."

Closer to his "western side of the hill" age than I care to admit, I find myself looking to the wisdom in Grandpa's poetry as I contemplate my own life, its challenges, and the changes I'm trying to make.

> Every one's a natural artist,
> Each has something he can do
> And if he can find his workshop
> He will make his dreams come true.

These words struck a chord in my heart and urged me to continue chasing my dreams, no matter how illusive (and elusive) they may seem. In rereading the poem in its entirety, I realized Grandpa was talking about the eternal creator in all of us, Soul.

The final stanza from "The Man Who Bends Over the Lathe" also captured my attention when I saw it in the newspaper clipping.

> No labor has ever been toilsome
> To the man who can make it an art
> For the hand never seems to grow weary
> When the work is attuned to the heart.

It was written about a man who was a machinist and clearly loved what he did. Grandpa admired that about him. I've been around people like that—who love what they do. And when you meet them, it's electrifying and inspiring. It doesn't matter if their passion is about washing machines, flint knapping, or adding turbo power to Audi A4s. When you're in the presence of that passion it is impossible not to glow just from being near one on fire.

And so as I set forth to write a new chapter in my life, though I am uncertain the outcome, I take direction from these two stanzas, certain that from one poet to another, my grandpa would not lead me astray.

Manifesting Dreams

Halloween costumes
not your average disguise
manifesting dreams

I STILL LOVE FABRIC STORES.

Of course, few, if any of them compare to the fabric store of my childhood. And that's not just because my imagination conjures memories of Hancock Fabric as a magical place, but because the nature of fabric sales has changed. People just don't sew like they used to. Nowadays, we can walk into any clothing store to buy super-affordable, ready-to-wear clothes. When I was growing up, it was cheaper to make one's own clothes and my mom frequently did.

Unlike lots of people with horrific stories of being scarred by having to wear clothes made by their mothers, I wore my handmade creations with pride. There was nothing, I mean ab-so-lutely nothing, my mom couldn't do with her sewing machine.

From everyday dresses, skirts, pants and tops, to duffle bags (I just got a compliment last fall on one I still use!), backpacks (I mean the serious backpacking kind, not just a day-use book bag), and new upholstery for my old 1962 Rambler. And prom dresses! I might have the design in mind, but Mom was the mastermind behind every formal dress I ever wore. I ADORED being able to create what I wanted—well, with Mom's expertise anyway.

But my love of the fabric store started earlier than the grade school through college clothing tales I regale you with here—it started with Halloween costumes when I was wee. They were always homemade. Raggedy Ann, replete with a yarn wig (So cool! Though it made my head itch and I hated that.), gypsy, ballerina, flapper, hobo.

Each costume started with an idea and a trip to Hancock's a few blocks away. My head would fill with visions of costumes, of something wonderful and new, never-before-seen. And there, amongst the forest of fabric we would wander, Mom and I, hunting for just the right thing. We always found it. And from nothing—thin air and thoughts—a costume, to help me become who I dreamed of being, would emerge.

This ability to envision something new and unique, then create it from nothing, well that's quite a life skill to pass along to one's daughter.

Thank you Mommy, for all the great costumes and clothes, hours in the fabric store and with the sewing machine, and most of all, sharing the love of creativity, creation, and transformation.

Popsicle Sticks

Mrs. McHenry's
popsicle-stick reward plan
carries forth today

MRS. MCHENRY was my first-grade teacher. She smelled like cigarettes and an unknown perfume. She scared me a little. I remember trying to learn to read in her class.

Stumped by a word, "It sounds like your name." She encouraged me.

Baffled, "Laura?" I couldn't figure out how the word in front of me could sound like my name.

Somewhat annoyed, "Your last name."

My five-year-old brain made the leap from Lee to, "Me!"

What hard work those early days of learning were.

Miss Jackson taught in the space next to Mrs. McHenry's class. It was a big open space with temporary walls that could be folded back, joining the rooms. Whereas my teacher had short hair, little make-up (save for the overly bright lipstick) and smelled funny, Miss Jackson had long, long hair she could sit on. She was glamorous looking and had violin-shaped bookends on her desk. She played in the symphony. Everybody loved Miss Jackson.

My mother had chosen Mrs. McHenry for me because my brother had been in her class. It was a well-known fact, Mrs. McHenry preferred boys. I would have chosen Miss Jackson.

Nevertheless, both teachers had a policy of rewarding us with popsicle sticks. They were painted and could be traded in for things like saf-t-pops™. There might have been other things we could get with them, but I only remember the lollipops and saving up my popsicle sticks.

In my memory, popsicle sticks were bestowed for doing good work and good deeds. It was the earliest reward system I remember and it has stuck with me.

For many years, I have had this idea that I am gleaning moments from my own life and collecting them like I did with Mrs. McHenry's popsicle sticks. It's not so much that I expect a reward, as I did when I was young, but that I wish to hold on to and cherish certain memories.

One such moment happened at the auto auction where I worked. Allow me to set the stage:

When I was a kid, this auction company had a showroom across from an amusement park called Legend City. Whenever we drove down to the airport, which wasn't terribly often, we would ogle over the cars in the lot as we waited to turn at the corner. My head would swivel around, taking them all in as we rounded the corner and I would ask Daddy questions about the cars I saw. Or, he might already be talking to my mom about one of the cars and I would listen intently.

One day when we approached the corner where the show-room was, Daddy pointed out a 1950, pale yellow, black ragtop Jeepster sitting in their lot. He used to have one just like that, called it the "Bumblebee," he said. I must have expressed enough interest that he pulled the car over so that we could get out and gaze at it through the chain-link fence.

I don't remember what he said about it—but I know there was joy and nostalgia in his voice. I took in the lines of the Jeep, the sunny color (that I couldn't imagine my dad picking out), and tried to imagine what it would be like to sit next to him, ragtop down, wind rushing. In that moment, I sent out a deep, heartfelt longing to the Universe, to someday take a ride with my dad in a car like that.

I truly believe, with all of my being, that the Universe hears all that we wish for and works to grant us those wishes. I also believe, that for those wishes to be granted, they must be for the best and highest good of everyone involved. And, the wish must be made from that place in our heart where deep, divine love resides.

I also believe that sometimes these things take a little time.

Perhaps even a lot of time.

Maybe even well over thirty years.

This year, as I was pulling memory chips from the video cameras during the check-in process for the auction, I walked out at just the right moment to catch a pale yellow, 1950 Jeepster with a black ragtop drive up.

It was scheduled to go up for sale on Sunday, the last day of the auction. The night before, I put a sticky note on the Jeepster's key bag that read:

> Jesse Lee won't say so,
> but he'd like to drive
> this car & his daughter
> would like to ride with him.

I knew the guys handing out keys the next morning would see the note and allow for this special request. (Normally, keys are handed out to whomever is next in line. Hanging back and trying to get a specific car is frowned on.) I knew, however, that since my dad never made requests like this, and had been working there for over two decades, the guys in charge of assigning cars would be okay with the request.

If I had tried, I couldn't have timed it any better. I hurried through my video duties Sunday morning hoping that I would make it over to the key control tent where they were assigning cars in time catch Daddy before he went to pick up the Jeepster. I walked up just as he was getting on a golf cart to be shuttled to lot number 1545.

What a thrill! Daddy looked pretty happy to see the black ragtop and "Springtime Yellow" vehicle. I rode shotgun with him up to the pre-staging area where cars are lined up before they go over the auction block.

While riding with him, I found out he had taken my mom

on their first date in that car. And then he told me about their first date. It made the ride with him even more special.

My husband had come out to Arizona towards the end of the auction, so I called him and asked if he could bring Mom out to the event. He said she seemed reluctant, but then I explained to him why it was important. Promising to do what he could to motivate my mom (if he couldn't do it, no one could, Mom loves my husband). Once the auction started, Daddy and I moved up to the front of pre-staging area, ready to head into the staging lanes.

Just before we needed to move the car again, my husband showed up with Mom and my brother (who happened to be passing through town at the same time we were there). Seeing my mom and dad next to the car—I couldn't help myself—the tears began to flow. (Part of it was having worked seventy-six hours in the last six days. Sheer exhaustion makes me emotional).

We encouraged Mom to ride up to the staging area with Daddy, which is when my brilliant photographer husband took a great shot of my parents smiling through the windshield.

I love this image because it's so easy for me to imagine my folks, twenty years younger than I am now, just stepping out into their lives together.

Mom got out of the car when we got up to staging and went to sit in the audience with my brother and husband. Grinning like a fool, I got into the car with Daddy as he drove it over the auction block.

I hold this experience close to my heart, hanging on to it like one of Mrs. McHenry's popsicle sticks—a reward for a long-awaited dream I'd nearly forgotten.

Before the Now

I remember him
Viking warrior adventures
from before the now

CARTOONS BECKONED, but I wanted a cohort this Saturday morning. As usual, I was up before everyone else. Either I'd been put to bed early, and had had enough of sleep, or my insomnia started as early as age three or four. In any case, the sun was up and so was I.

I went into my brother Jimmy's bedroom. Sunlight powered through the closed slats of the shutters in the windows. It was early, but the sun was bright, so it must have been summer, maybe the summer before I went to kindergarten, when I was four.

My presence next to his bed woke him and I asked if he wanted to come watch cartoons with me. Before he uttered his response, time stopped.

I noticed a smattering of pale freckles across his nose. His eyes were an infinite blue, one I would later recognize as Prussian blue in a painting class. I looked into those eyes and I remembered. *I know you*, a part of me whispered. So this is what you look like now.

I erupted into squeals of laughter when Jimmy attacked me in a tickle fest. I folded the timeless moment up into a neat origami package corking it into a bottle I floated to my future self. A self that existed at the same moment as others, not somewhere down a linear now, but a now that is held in each moment, the eternal now.

Years later, somewhere amidst my twenties, I would command myself to awaken in a dream. Lucid, I rounded a corner where I was met by twelve of my past lives, the first of which was a tall Viking warrior. When I shared the dream with Jimmy, he confided he'd felt drawn to Vikings.

"Maybe that's one of the places we know each other from." The words were out of my mouth without the intervention of my mind. I knew I'd hit upon a truth.

I also knew that the *where* of the past life didn't matter. What mattered was that we had the opportunity to be together again.

That Saturday morning in early childhood, I recognized in Jimmy his eternal self, soul, wearing a new costume for this lifetime. This allowed me to register the same divine legacy in myself and extend it further—we all exist from before the now.

Childlike Joy

just for a moment
transported to childlike joy
of Christmas morning

CHRISTMAS. Ahh … but it was magical.

I could hardly go to sleep. I wanted it to be morning so badly. Finally, sometime in the middle of the night, I would creep down the hallway, afraid I might catch Santa in the act, and I didn't want to be relegated to the "bad kid" list. So I would reach around the corner of the bookcase where we hung our stockings. If they were full, then I'd know the coast was clear; Santa had been there and I would be able to take a peek at what he'd brought.

In our house, Santa didn't wrap presents. He would carefully arrange all my gifts in a special area, like a chair, or an end of the sofa. Santa did this for everyone in my family. He also filled the stockings. The years I was old enough to have the nerve and thought to do so, I would sneak into the kitchen to find a flashlight so I could peek at what he'd brought.

Santa always brought books. I can't remember a Christmas

I didn't get a book (or a set of books). *Little House in the Big Woods*, *Gone with the Wind*, *Little Women*, *A Wrinkle in Time* (and the rest in the series), *The Earthsea Trilogy* ... so many papery tickets to adventure. And the thoughtful gifts!

One of the most standout from my childhood: A wonderful toy kitchen my mother had carefully constructed from boxes and contact paper. A stove, sink and sideboard! Pure enchantment. The sink was a box with a yellow plastic bowl that fit into an opening in the top of the box. It was marvelously clever! I still have the stove—upside down, it is the box that holds treasures from my childhood.

Christmas last year was spent in the company of my husband's family. His nephew was nine. His mother, my husband's sister, thought this might be the final year he truly believed in Santa Claus and had gone all out with the presents.

My husband and I didn't have kids. For the most part, I don't regret this decision. But at Christmas and Halloween, I sometimes wish differently. On Christmas Eve, after my nephew had set out cookies and milk for Santa, carrots for the reindeer, and reluctantly trudged off to bed, we helped my husband's sister set up for the next morning. It was such a treat to be Santa's helper.

As a chronic insomniac, it's not unusual for me to wake at all hours of the morning and be unable to go back to sleep. This was one such morning. When my nephew woke and wanted to go downstairs to see if Santa had arrived, I was filled with the same excitement as I had in childhood.

My husband grumbled about the time, (somewhere between five and six) and I poked him, reminding him that this was a special time. I didn't mind getting up at all. In fact, I egged my nephew on, whipping up the excitement as I got out of bed and into my robe as quickly as possible to meet him on the landing.

Both the tree and the small "Morning Room" where it stood had been decked with as many lights and ornaments as possible and was burgeoning with festivity. I stood at the base of the stairs and watched as my nephew approached the room. It was in that moment, I was transported, with all the love and wonder and magic and bliss, to the heart of my childhood Christmas. It was so palpable, so lovely and tangible. I bathed the fresh memory with tears and reached for a tissue, tucking that dear sweet experience into my heart with all the joy of the season.

Whatever you celebrate this season or in life, I hope it brings you the fresh awe and wonder of a child.

Beloved Memory

Shadows and Sunshine
a book by my grandfather
poetry in bloom

"H EY GAL!" He calls to me as I step through the shadow
of the pines that surround the lake to meet him on
the brief sandy beach at Redfish Lake. We're on the opposite
end of the lake from the lodge. I can see the red log siding
of it across the way. The fishing is better here, Grandpa
explains. "Here" is a lake in the heart of the Sawtooth Moun-
tains of Idaho. We visit this place nearly every summer. I
squint up at him and smile, not yet self conscious of the
yawning gap between my two front teeth.

I'm seven, I think, maybe a year older or a year younger. My
hair is short, boy short, and I hate that because people often
call me a boy. But that's the hair cut chosen by my mother,
who wants nothing to do with snarls, tangles and complaints
that might accompany her having to comb out my unruly,
thick locks. I won't grow my hair long until I'm ten and my
mother has been assured I can take care of it myself. For

now I wear the popular Dorothy Hamill haircut, ubiquitous across America on girls of all ages. I stick one hip out, putting my weight on it as I inspect one of the numerous mosquito bites on my arm.

A few feet away Grandpa baits up my hook with salmon eggs. They're bright red. Too brightly red to be a natural color, but I don't know that at the time. "We'll try this first and see how that does," he tells me as he puts the pole in my hands positioning them correctly.

He doesn't let go, but instead stands behind me, patient and steady, smelling of aftershave and the Brach's Star Bright peppermints that he so loves. With a swing of our arms to the right, then forward, I feel his finger press down on mine, releasing the catch on the reel at just the right time so the line is freed and unreels out into the lake. A satisfying wet plop sounds as the spherical red and white plastic floater hits the water. Behind me, Grandpa brings up an aluminum, folding chair sized just for me. He buries part of the legs in the sand to steady it and I flop down carelessly. I dig my toes into the sand, notice that it's cooler and more damp below, and flick them back out of the holes I've dug. The sun is at our backs, reflecting blinding brightness on the water. I look over at Grandpa as he prepares his own pole with some salmon eggs and casts out as well.

"You keep the tip of your rod up there, Gal," he reminds me as he scoots his own aluminum folding chair next to mine and we settle in.

There are a few motorboats out on the lake, but not many;

it's still fairly early. That's the best time to fish, Grandpa says, when the fish are still hungry. We've got a net, three poles, a tackle box, a box of worms, and a metal basket we'll tie to a bush near the lake so we can put it in the water, keeping the fish alive after we've caught them. I listen to the quiet laps on the shore caused by a boat out in the middle of the lake.

Grandpa starts to recite one of his poems. He does that sometimes. I find it kind of funny and wonder if other people's grandpas recite their poetry at random times. His voice is deep, and I look at his profile as he recites his poem to me and the lake and the trout. He wears glasses and a Stetson; his steady gaze is far out across the water, far away from here, in the place where the poetry comes from. I follow his words there, though I really don't know what they mean. They are the sound of Grandpa, the lake, the wind. The birds join in and the sun rises higher. I sit up in my chair and check to make sure the tip of my rod is up—I don't want to disappoint Grandpa by letting it drop.

He finishes his recitation, makes a sucking sound as he plays with his dentures, then looks over at me. "How ya doin' there, Gal?"

I brighten and check the tip of the pole again. "Good!" I grin the jack-o-lantern-tooth grin.

"Good." He nods out towards the lake. "We're gonna catch some good ones today, Gal." He sucks his dentures again and chuckles.

We sit for a while. We sit for what feels like ages to

me. When Grandpa looks over, he knows my spirits have drooped with the pole, "Reel in your line, Gal!" He booms.

I jump a little bit, momentarily thinking I've let the unthinkable happen: I've let the pole hit the sand in my bored stupor.

"We're gonna get you a fish on that line!" he commands of me and the fish and the lake.

Relieved, I reel in my line, slow and steady, just like he's taught me. When he grabs the bobber I can see that my salmon eggs are gone. "Did you feel a tug on there?"

"No sir." Not so sure. "I don't think so." I think about it some more. "Maybe a tiny one?"

"Must be extra hungry to steal your eggs without letting you know." He reaches for the box of worms. "We'll fix this up. Maybe they want worms for breakfast more than eggs." He winks at me deflating in the aluminum chair.

As he casts out for me he says, "I'm gonna put this right in front of the fish's mouth for ya."

I smile into pale blue of his twinkling eyes as he hands me the pole. "Okay." Not sure that's really possible. But he's a grandpa, so maybe …

He doesn't even have time to pick up his own pole, which had been placed in a holder by his chair, when I squeal with delight. I can feel it! There is a distinct tug on my line that says to me, "Hey! I'm here! I'm alive!"

Grandpa looks over to see the line pulled hard and taut on the end of my pole, bending it down a substantial amount. He's as excited as I am as he shouts instructions on how to handle the pole and line. There is a dance of give and take, and my small arms start to tire. Grandpa is the greatest cheerleader though, keeping me strong. Together we reel in a fine cutthroat trout on my line, his words, and the sunshine between us.

&

struggling to draw out
a consistency of form
rearranging dreams

I HELD TWO PENCILS in my hand. I'd banded them together so that when I drew, the two lead lines formed the outside edges of a calligraphic letter—a fantastic trick I'd learned while practicing lettering in a calligraphy class.

The letter M crooked its serifed left leg at me. "Psst …" It waggled. "I've got something for you here."

I ignored the M and moved on to the W. I wanted to letter a friend's birthday card envelope with two standout initials. I needed to stay focused. I didn't have much time.

"Listen," the M implored, "this isn't about me." M grinned in the way that's been ascribed to it: deeply, with a pointy lower lip and continued, "It's about Amp. You need to start making a new ampersand."

I shrugged the annoying fly of a thought away.

But my flypaper brain snagged it anyway.

My current ampersand, the backwards 3 with the vertical

lines above and below it, was somewhat lacking in grace. Not that my handwriting is beautifully flowing. It's generally more blocky, bold, and entirely uppercased. Except when it's more scribbly and cramped: all dangly y's, j's and g's dipping into the unknown with elevated l's, f's and h's reaching for more. It depends on what I'm writing. But in either case, my ampersand seemed an anachronism among its lettered cronies. Everyone else had matured and moved on. Amp however, had stayed put, hovering somewhere around the sixth grade.

I heeded the nudge for a new ampersand. The next few months of journaling saw varied success with this endeavor. The backwards 3 was replaced with something that looked more like the flowing &. Well, sometimes it flowed; many times it didn't.

Six months into the new ampersand experiment, I recently journaled:

> It's not so much that I feel lost, as sort of …
> unsure & slightly disconnected, like there is
> a rearranging going on.

Suddenly,
the need for a new symbol
of addition
made more sense.
Yes &
This & that
Then & now

I'm still struggling
with the consistency
of my form.
Consistency comes with practice
which eventually
earns mastery

&

About the ampersand I penned:
I wanted something more
the turn of a page
I saw the phrase
could be the whole:

I wanted something more.

&

Mellifluous is the word
I wanted to add next.
But the page,
well, looking back at it,
there was room
for the word
on the other page,
but it felt too crowded

&

I wanted more
more room
more space
the change of a fresh page

&

I was unsure
about the word choice—
I thought of mellifluous
as pertaining to sound.
As I considered
the possible correlation
and application,
I turned the page

&

I noticed my hanging phrase
felt it had
meat and merit
enough of its own.
I wanted something more.
But still ...
mellifluous beckoned

&

I opened up my favorite app,
the one I use so much
it's in my phone's dock
(where boats are kept
before setting sail
... but I digress.)

Webster's says
1. Having a smooth rich flow.

Yes, please!

&

&

That's when I sat up.
Astonished.
Three days ago I was stung by a bee.
Honey.
The sweetness of life.

&

In the moments before the sting,
I'd been working on this book,
collaborating with my husband on its layout

&

daydreaming about a life with a better fit
a shoe that allowed
a more comfortable stride

&

cadence to our creativity
more sweetness
more honey

&

I thanked the bee for its stinger
its zinger
a reminder

&

amongst the resulting itch
the image of one tiny change
one backwards 3
with daggers above

&

below
consciously changed

&

with fresh movements
a new conjunction
a new addition
a rearranging

&

an ever unfolding
the architecture
of our lives

&

dreams

&

a recognition of this movement
this symbol

all the love around us.

Gratitude

releasing long-held
millennia-old judgments
making room for love

EVERY BOOK has its own long road to creation. It's taken me my entire adulthood to embrace myself as a writer. Longer still if you count the times before the Now. In any case, I worked hard to release long-held, millennia-old judgments heaped upon myself to get to this sentence.

THANK YOU.

Thank you to Daddy, for asking when I would publish something and Mom for always enjoying my work. It never occurred to me to self-publish until Jay planted the seed—thank you! To my trio of adventuresome editors: Bethie, Barbara and Lois, endless gratitude for your eagle eyes and gift of time. Thank you to all my friends who kept me on track with their queries about the book's progress. Special thanks to Susie for The Blurb and to Sheri for empowering me to publish just because.

How to thank my husband Seth? The first ear to hear clunkers and potential, celebrating each completion, being my champion, voice of reason, and book designer. Just as you have touched every part of my life, your touch, your presence is embedded in every line of this book. I could not have done this with out your love, support and uncanny ability to learn and absorb new-to-you computer programs. Thank you will never suffice—across space and time ...

And most of all, thank you kind reader for joining me on this journey.

For Lovers of Details

Unemployment = Opportunity
Unemployment = Opportunity haiku and beginning of essay 2014, essay conclusion 2020
Curator haiku and essay 2012. At the time they were written, I was reading and inspired by Sarah Ban Breathnach's book *Simple Abundance*.
Surrender haiku and essay 2014
Sotto Voce haiku and essay 2012
Paperbirds first haiku August 2011, second haiku November 2011, third haiku January 2012, essay May 2012
Automotive Confection haiku and essay 2013
To Volunteer haiku and essay 2013
Beyond the Target haiku and essay 2015
About Rest haiku 2007, essay 2013

Nature
Sidewalk Flowers haiku and essay 2018
Yearning haiku and essay 2013
Maple Syrup haiku and essay 2014
Idyllic haiku and essay 2014
A Name haiku and essay 2014
Introducing Lotta haiku and essay 2020

Pure Quirk
Slippery Fish haiku and essay 2015
Absolute Detachment haiku and essay 2016
MARBLE/marble haiku 2007, essay 2006
Reality first haiku and essay 2012, second haiku 2010

For Lovers of Details

The Exuberance haiku and essay 2016

All the Love Around Us
Lifeboat haiku 2010, essay 2012
Falling in Love first haiku and essay 2012, second haiku 2008 during the road trip with my sister
Steel Steed haiku and essay 2013
Heart of an Explorer haiku and essay 2014
A Poet haiku and essay 2012
Manifesting Dreams haiku and essay 2014
Popsicle Sticks haiku and essay 2014
Before the Now haiku 2019, essay 2020
Childlike Joy haiku and essay 2014
Beloved Memory haiku 2007, essay 2010
& haiku and essay 2020

Gratitude
Gratitude haiku 2020

Timeline of Places
2007–2008 Boulder, Colorado
2008–2009 Scottsdale, Arizona
2009–2012 Boulder/Denver, Colorado
2012–2014 Topsfield, Massachusetts
2014–2015 Scottsdale, Arizona
Summer 2015 Rochester, Vermont
2015–2021 Scottsdale/Phoenix, Arizona

About the Author

LALEE BOND writes in the margins of her life and full-time job at a small museum in a large archaeological park that's tucked in the heart of Phoenix, Arizona, where she lives with her husband, Seth, and their cat, Bella the Tikken. *The Love Around Us* is her first book.

To join her Haiku Thursday list (receive a haiku every Thursday—sometimes silly, sometimes thoughtful, always a seventeen-syllable slice of life), discover more haiku (with photos!), or contact the author, visit www.LauraLeeBond.com.

Made in the USA
Las Vegas, NV
28 December 2021

39711344R00144